Meet the 7 Retir

1. **LADY LONGEVITY:** Of course we all want to live a long, healthy life; but Lady Longevity puts an evil spin on our wish. Her goal is to try to make you ignore the possibility of a long life in your retirement plan, thereby leaving you penniless and without choices if you outlive your money! Truly evil!

2. **THE INVISIBLE ENEMY:** This photo is of one of the rare occasions he allowed us to see him – because normally he remains completely hidden. He is inflation, and his goal is to make things FAR more expensive the longer you live – ruining your retirement lifestyle!

3. **EVIL UNCLE SAM:** We all know that we need to pay taxes to the IRS, but Evil Uncle Sam goes a step further. He looks for all the different ways he can squeeze more and more money out of retirees. These taxes often don't affect the rich OR the poor. Instead, he goes after the people who work their whole lives to try to save for a comfortable retirement: You and me!

Turn the Page for the Other 4 Retirement Villains!

4. SARAH SELF-PAY: Sure, our government provides retirees with Medicare; but what about all the types of illnesses Medicare *doesn't* cover? Nursing care can cost up to $7,000 a month or even more! Sarah Self-Pay's goal is to force you to pay ALL of that out of your savings…until there's nothing left!

5. ICEBERG IVAN: Ivan pulls the fees out of your savings and investments. Like the "tip of the iceberg," he tries to make sure you can't see them. His goal is to cost you hundreds of thousands of dollars during your retirement, all the while keeping those fees hidden under the surface and out of sight!

6. SYSTEMATIC SAMMY: Sammy poses as a financial planner and gives you what sounds like a logical plan for you to take income systematically from your nest egg during your retirement. Little do you suspect that his "plan" could destroy your nest egg faster than you can say "a wolf in sheep's clothing!"

7. ANTIQUATED ANDY: At first glance, Andy may seem harmless; but he represents out-dated investment strategies that many Wall Street firms refuse to update. These strategies could expose your nest egg to many unnecessary risks. A true hazard to your *wealth!*

Save Your Retirement!

PAT STRUBBE

Out to Save Your Retirement From Mass Destruction By The 7 Retirement Villains!

ISBN-10: 1463769377
ISBN-13: 978-1463769376

DEDICATION

To my wife and children:

Janelle: Your unfailing love and commitment are my rock.
Your support means the world to me.

Carter and Ava: You are the light of my life,
and I grow more proud of you every day.

Contents

ABOUT THE AUTHOR

Widely recognized in South Carolina and beyond, Patrick A. Strubbe, ChFC, CLU, RFC is the founder and owner of Preservation Specialists, LLC. His mission is to help his clients retire with confidence. He believes retirement should be about being able to do what you want, when you want, with whom you want – all on your own terms.

He has fifteen years experience specializing in retirement planning, and has been featured in the Columbia Business Monthly and Senior Market Advisor. Since October 2009, he has been the monthly finance columnist for the Lexington County Chronicle.

After growing up in Indiana, Pat graduated with honors from Purdue University, and lives in Columbia with his wife Janelle and kids Carter and Ava.

Introduction

I'll never forget the first time I saw the difficulties of handling your finances in retirement. I was 16. As you might imagine, retirement financial planning wasn't something that I was typically on my mind!

This story is about my friendship with my grandpa. He was my mom's dad, and since my grandmother had died when I was a baby, he had been a widower for many years by the time I was a teenager.

My grandpa was a farmer. While he'd served his country in the military for many years, including duty in World War II and Korea, even as a little boy I knew he was a farmer. I was raised in northern Indiana, and grandpa lived in the southeast part of the state - a whole 'nother world to me!

My parents, sister, and I traveled down to southeast Indiana a couple times a year to visit grandpa and other relatives. I vividly remember what we'd do *every* time we saw my grandpa: we'd take a walk on his farmland. He loved to do that. So we did – every time.

In fact, there's one specific moment I remember from when I was about four. There was a particular area of his land that was completely fenced in, and we pulled up in our car to his gate. He couldn't open the gate that day, so everyone was climbing over it. It was about 5 feet high, but as soon as I saw my older sister climb that fence by herself, gosh darn it I was determined to climb it too! When grandpa tried to help me, I was adamant: "No, grandpa, I can do it myself!"

Okay, I have to admit something here: the reason I remember that moment so clearly is because my grandpa thought it was hilarious;

and he loved to tell that story! Every time he did we had a good laugh over it. Even now it always brings a smile to my face.

By the time I was a teenager, my grandpa's health had declined considerably. After a series of mini-strokes, he simply couldn't live by himself anymore. There was no way he would ever consider moving away from his hometown, so moving in with us wasn't an option. That meant a nursing care facility.

Now remember, as a teenager I was completely oblivious to how those nursing care bills were being paid. All I knew was that instead of heading to grandpa's house to visit him, we would go to his nursing care facility.

My Sixteenth Birthday

As he did on all my other birthdays, my grandpa called me on my 16th. We had a nice talk, and then he dropped his big surprise on me: for my sixteenth birthday he wanted to buy me a new car! Wow! I couldn't have been more excited! As nice as it had been in all the previous years to receive a card with a few dollars in it, you can imagine how much more excited I was about this!

After we were done on the phone, grandpa talked with my mom. She was a CPA and is a very shrewd financial person, and she was handling all my grandpa's bills.

After she finished the phone call, mom sat me down, looked me square in the eye, and told me that grandpa couldn't buy me a car. I was in disbelief! How could I go from no expectation of a car, to a promise of a brand new car, back to no car at all in the space of less than an hour?!

I couldn't understand why there was a problem. As far as I knew, my grandpa had never had any financial problems. If he says he's going to buy me a car, why wouldn't he be able to?

This is when I got my first lesson in working with finances in retirement. My mom explained that before his health declined, my grandpa had never had money problems. He lived comfortably in 'retirement' for many years with income coming in from Social Security, his military pension, and income from his farm.

But when grandpa had his medical problems his financial situation changed overnight. His monthly expenses skyrocketed. And while he had plenty of assets (his farmland), he of course didn't have an endless supply of cash in the bank. Not only are nursing care facilities costly, but it's often difficult to predict future costs that might arise. Plus, his house was on his farmland, so there were still monthly expenses there.

It was hard for the family to deal with my grandpa's health problems. But that's when I realized just how hard it was to deal with the financial problems too. On top of figuring out everything with regard to healthcare for my grandpa, (from a long distance no less) my mom had to deal with the stress of managing his finances and assets to pay for his nursing care and other monthly bills.

My grandpa passed away when I was in college. I started school as an accounting major because I knew I liked math, and I liked money. ☺ But his situation always stayed in my mind. I was blessed to graduate from Purdue University during a strong economy, and I had five job offers to pick from.

I choose to help people with their finances; and after two years devouring all the basics, I found a mentor to teach me all about the details of helping people as they plan their retirement and throughout their retirement. Ever since then, I've focused on being the best planner focusing on the retirement years that I can be. I'm so fortunate to have found the area I love so quickly in life, and that passion is why I wrote this book.

You see, there's nothing I get more satisfaction out of than when I make a difference in a client's life. But I believe that as difficult as retirement planning is today, it is going to get tougher and tougher. Over the coming pages, we'll talk about why in more detail. In his powerful book *But What If I Live?,* author Gregory Salsbury, Ph.D. sums this up very well:

> *"Every successive generation of Americans over the last century has been more prosperous and has enjoyed a better quality of life and a better retirement. Every generation has seen an improvement – until now. But at the same time, retirement didn't used to be a problem – until now. To paraphrase a line from Oldsmobile, "This is not your parents' retirement." The trouble is many boomers don't seem to know that retirement, if we have one, may be inferior to their parents', yet no one seems worried. And no one is taking action."*

Mr. Salsbury is absolutely right. Now more than ever, Americans need straight talk on where they stand financially; and they need help getting where they want to go. That's why I love what I do, and that's why I wrote this book. My hope is that it helps you Save *YOUR* Retirement!

Chapter 1

The REAL Reason Your Retirement Needs to Be Saved!

Ohnosis: Realizing that you really should have started planning for retirement years ago.

Retirementology, by Gregory Salsbury, Ph.D.

In 1974 the Employee Retirement Income Security Act (ERISA) was passed.[1] This law birthed the IRA (Individual Retirement Account) and set the groundwork for any and all accounts we now know today as "retirement accounts."

The intent of ERISA was to encourage us to save for our own retirement. You could say that a very simple summary of ERISA's goal for us was for each person to have 3 areas to lean on in retirement:

1. Social Security
2. A Worker's Own Savings
3. A Company Pension Plan

This is often referred to as the "3 legged stool of retirement planning." On May 5th, 2002, an article in the Washington Post titled

"Pension Changes Pose Challenges" made some important observations about this retirement stool:

> *Last time we looked, the first leg, Social Security, was still standing, though shuddering a bit as its guarantees are pecked away at- ever-increasing taxable income, a raised retirement age, taxation of some benefits and so forth…*
>
> *All the lettered and numbered savings plans blessed by Congress-the 401(k)s, 403(b)s, IRAs, SEP-IRAs, Keoghs- were arguably intended to bolster the second leg, workers' savings, needed to meet an ever longer and ever more expensive retirement. The corporate tax benefits attached to the company-sponsored plans- made up largely of worker's own cash-have been nudged over to bolster or even replace the third leg of the stool. Instead of rewarding thrift in employees, they have enabled companies to ditch or severely curtail traditional pension plans.*
>
> *All of which means: Look, Ma, a three-legged stool with only two legs!*

Let's back up and take a good look at this. So before ERISA, a successful retirement depended on payments from Social Security and from your company pension plan. It sounds pretty straightforward. It also sounds pretty secure. In fact, you could say that an employee could retire and confidently expect their check to be in the mail. But with the introduction of the retirement plans that ERISA paved the way for, now we are responsible for a portion of that security.

The author makes an interesting observation: companies realized that these very retirement plans gave them the opportunity to reduce or even eliminate the expensive pension plans they had been providing. And who can blame them? Dropping pension plans saves companies billions of dollars every year. When ERISA was passed, we were told it was to benefit employees. However, employ***ers*** have benefited in a lot of ways. In many cases the expense of retirement has been transferred from the employ***er*** to the employ***ee.***

The Incredible Disappearing Pension!

Maybe you're thinking, "Oh I'm sure it's not that bad - maybe just a couple big companies that have done away with their plans." That is sadly far from true. In fact, *an astounding more than 1,000 employers voluntarily shut down their defined benefit pension plans each and every year!*[2] Want further proof that the defined benefit pension plan is going the way of the dinosaur? Take a look at the number of active pension plans. In 1985, 114,396 defined benefit plans were active. In 2003, that number had dropped to 29,512.[3] That's a remarkable drop of 74%! Harvard University Law professor Elizabeth Warren cut to the chase when she said *"There's no business in America that isn't going to figure out a way to get rid of (these benefit promises.)"*[4]

Why are these companies doing this? Because they need to, and because they can!

<u>Because they need to</u>: Over 50% of the 100 biggest corporate defined benefit pensions were under-funded in 2002.[5] So how does the company fix that problem? They can either pore piles of money into their pension plan, or they can weasel their way out of making the payments. Which of these options do you think they'll choose?

<u>Because they can</u>: Numerous companies have already succeeded at reducing or completely eliminating their pension commitments. So a company that has a problem today can learn from those that have had that problem (and used this solution!) in the past.

The most widely known option is declaring bankruptcy. It's happened time and time again over the past decade. A large corporation declares bankruptcy. Part of this process is pleading with a bankruptcy judge to allow the company to void its union contracts. One major reason for this? To reduce or eliminate the existing pension commitments!

But wait, you say, doesn't the government have a program to protect us from these evil companies trying to weasel their way out of their pension promises? You're right. Most defined benefit pension plans are insured by the Pension Benefit Guaranty Corporation (PBGC). However, I'm sure you know that this program has its limits just like anything else.

For example, in 2004, the PBGC had $62.3 *billion* in long term obligations and a deficit of $23 *billion.*[6] Of course, things have only gotten worse since then! The Congressional Budget Office estimated that the PBGC deficit will increase to $86.7 billion by 2015, and to $141.9 billion by 2025.[7]

The bottom line is that there is no reason for us to believe that the PBGC will be able to cover all the reduced and eliminated pension benefits out there. They actually don't always pay the full benefit anyway. In some existing cases, *benefits have been cut by 60 to 70%!*[8] So much for being insured!

What About Public Pensions?

Sadly, corporate pensions aren't the only ones with huge problems. In August 2010, the Government Accountability Office (GAO) delivered a report titled "State and Local Government Pension Plans" to the Ranking Member of the U.S. Senate Committee on Finance. It reported that the average public pension plan holds assets that are less than 85% of the current value of future liabilities. That means there's on average a 15% difference between what they SHOULD have to cover those pensions and what they ACTUALLY have.

In 2009, Robert Novy-Marx, professor at the University of Chicago, and Joshua D. Rauh, professor at Northwestern University, presented a paper titled "The Liabilities and Risks of the State-Sponsored Pension Plans." The authors analyzed the 116 largest state pension plans and found a frightening shortfall. Based on reports prepared by the pension plans themselves, the present value of liabilities at the end of 2008 was estimated to be $2.98 trillion; but the assets in the plans at that point were only $1.94 trillion – which means they had only 65% of the proper funding!

West Virginia, Illinois and Philadelphia are scary examples – and show that neither cities nor states are immune to this problem. In the April 4th, 2011 issue of Bloomberg Businessweek, Roger Lowenstein reviews public pensions in detail in his article: "The Great American Ponzi Scheme." (Yes, the title of the article is referring to public pensions!)

The article reports that Illinois pensions are currently funded at only 51%, Philadelphia's at 47%, and West Virginia's at an incredible 43%. Yes, that means based on current assumptions, Philadelphia and West Virginia have saved *less than half* of what they should have to cover their pension obligations!

Do you think that municipalities will always find a way to pay their pensions? Not true. In the same article, Lowenstein reports that Prichard, Alabama was forced to stop sending retirees their checks in 2010.

But we were supposed to have a 3 legged stool, right? Once they take away the pension leg, now we're down to two legs. Oh, and that's assuming we trust Social Security. Yikes! We went from an idea of 3 legs to 2, one of which is teetering.

Social Insecurity

I'm sure you've heard time and time again about the problems with Social Security, but this is a REAL problem and warrants attention. Let me quickly make a few points.

First, the government is brilliant at making it sound like we've been 'saving' all the excess taxes to fund Social Security over the years. They make it sound like our Social Security taxes go into a Social Security Trust Fund. This couldn't be further from the truth.

Instead, part of the taxes received are used to pay current Social Security benefits. The remaining tax revenue is put into the general revenue fund to be used as the government sees fit. There are NO assets in a trust fund – therefore there is NO interest on the trust fund. This tax revenue is accounted for by the Secretary of the Treasury issuing an IOU for the amount that is used in the general fund. By the end of 2009, the U.S. government owes the trust fund approximately $2.5 *Trillion.* That's not a made up number from someone making projections. That comes straight from the 2010 Social Security Trustees Report!

Ready for more bad news? Recent projections had us believe that Social Security revenue would be greater than expenses until somewhere around 2016. It turns out, we hit the mark a little sooner than expected…in 2010! The title of analyst Michael Barone's article in the Washington Examiner says it all:

> "Social Security Cash Flow Suddenly Negative"
>
> *Social Security tax receipts for the first half of 2010: $346.9 billion; Social Security benefits payments for the same period: $347.3 billion. Before this year, projections have always been that Social Security wouldn't cross that line into negative cash flow for five years or so. Now it's a reality. Congress has been spending Social Security's positive cash flow for years. Now there's no positive cash flow to spend.*[9]

So what is the only leg left? Our savings. And do you know what is one of the craziest parts of the whole situation? What ERISA ultimately ended up doing was forcing millions of employees to become professional investors and financial planners – requiring us to handle building this savings on our own…without providing us with the financial education needed to plan successfully! Instead of finding a way to educate investors, the politicians have left the job of financial education up to the people of Wall Street.

Does that sound like a good idea? I think best-selling author Robert T. Kiyosaki of Rich Dad, Poor Dad fame said it best in his book *Rich Dad's Prophecy*:

> *"Asking Wall Street to provide financial education is the same as asking a fox to raise your chickens."*

But that's what we've been forced to do. After all, when you were in school, you were taught all kinds of things, right? Maybe you were taught Latin, for example, or trigonometry, or studied Shakespeare.

But when and where did anyone teach us how to take care of ourselves and plan for our financial future? Who taught us how to deal with the real financial issues that face us today?

It doesn't matter if you're a blue collar worker, a business owner, a top corporate executive…or anything in between, most of us are not taught how to take care of ourselves financially, or how to plan for taxes and inflation, or how to figure out what we need to do to meet our goals, or how to deal with the reality of paying mortgages, bills, tax problems, wildly fluctuation stock and bond markets, cash flows, budgeting, insurance, long-term care, health care costs, and on and on and on.

This is not typically taught in our school systems. So let's go back to Robert Kiyosaki's comment:

"Asking Wall Street to provide financial education is the same as asking a fox to raise your chickens."

Who is the fox Mr. Kiyosaki is referring to? That would be many of the financial salespeople you run into. Amazingly, stockbrokers from some of the biggest brokerage firms in the United States have even said they are not financial advisors or planners, but merely commission compensated salespeople whose primary job is to sell financial products! Where did they say this? *In sworn testimony!* (The brokers sued their employers under the Fair Labor Standards Act. Under Fact Sheet 17M stockbrokers are entitled to overtime pay if their primary duty is selling financial products.)[10]

Interestingly, at the same time these stockbrokers are saying they're just salespeople, the brokerage industry is spending billions of dollars every year on advertising; and what titles do they use for their representatives in those ads? Here's a sampling:

- Financial Advisor[11]
- Investment Advisor[12]

Sounds to me like the brokerage firms don't think it would come off very well if their advertisements said something like: "Come in and meet with us – we've got the best salespeople in the country!"

The U.S. Securities and Exchange Commission has taken a stand here as well. They require all brokerage statements to display this message:

Your account is a brokerage account and not an advisory account. Our interests may not always be the same as yours. Please ask questions to make sure you understand your rights and our obligations to you, including the extent of our obligations to disclose conflicts of interest and to act in your best interests. We are paid both by you and sometimes by people who compensate us based on what you buy from us. Therefore, our profits and our salespersons' compensations may vary by product and over time.[13]

We should all beware the fox chasing after the chickens!

Mr. Kiyosaki has one other piece of advice I must pass on:

> *"The point I want to reinforce is the idea that you as an individual have 3 basic choices:*
>
> *(1) Do nothing,*
>
> *(2) Follow the same old financial planning advice of diversify, or*
>
> *(3) Get financially educated.*
>
> *The choice is yours. Obviously, I recommend long-term financial education."*

I couldn't have said it better myself! I hope you now understand WHY your retirement needs to be saved. That's why I wrote this book. Over the last 15 years, I've met with thousands of people to discuss their retirement plans. It pains me to see so many who aren't prepared.

Instead of giving you a boring textbook on steps to take to protect your retirement, what follows is a story. It includes:

- A couple planning for retirement: Dick and Jane
- Their friends who have already successfully planned for their retirement: Tommy and Brenda
- 7 retirement villains who you will meet throughout the rest of this book, and, of course,
- Our superhero: SuperRetirementPlanner

What did you expect, Superman? ☺ I hope you enjoy, and I hope you plan and retire with confidence!

END NOTES

1. www.DOL.gov/ebsa
2. But What if I Live, Gregory B. Salsbury, 2006
3. "The Really Troubled Program," Time Magazine, January 4, 2005
4. "The Great Retirement Ripoff: The Broken Promise," Time Magazine, October 31, 2005
5. "Report Finds Underfunding at Largest U.S. Pensions," Insurance Newscast, June 2, 2005
6. Mary Williams Walsh, "Whoops! There Goes Another Pension Plan," The New York Times, September 19, 2005
7. Mary Williams Walsh, "Whoops! There Goes Another Pension Plan," The New York Times, September 19, 2005
8. Savita Iyer, "PBGC Releases Pension Benefit Guarantee for 2006 and Retirement Age Table," InvestmentAdvisor.com, December 20, 2005
9. "Social Security Cash Flow Suddenly Negative," The Washington Examiner, June 12, 2010
10. The Lies About Money, Ric Edelson, 2007
11. http://fa.smithbarney.com/
12. http://www.totalmerrill.com/TotalMerrill/pages/accolades.aspx?pageurl=THE_BUCK_GROUP
13. The Lies About Money, Ric Edelson, 2007

Chapter 2

The Aging of America

By 2030, the demographics of 32 states will resemble those of Florida today.

Gregory Salsbury, PhD ,*But What If I Live?*

Our story begins on a beautiful sunny day in Metropolis. Meet residents of Metropolis, Dick and Jane. Dick is 55 and Jane is 53. Jane works part time as a receptionist at a dental office. Dick is an engineer. While he likes his job, he dreams of having the freedom to do what he wants, when he wants. So he is planning feverishly for retirement.

Dick has spent the last few years devouring Money magazine, CNBC, the money section of USA Today, and personal finance articles he has found on Google. He has studied his pension benefits from his employer, poured money into his 401k, and estimated his social security benefits. Overall, he's a do-it-yourselfer, and in many ways he's done a thorough job.

Dick has decided it's time to show his plan to Jane. They sat in their den where Dick had been working and re-working his numbers for years. "Honey," Dick started, "I've crunched all the numbers, and the great news is, between my pension, our social security benefits, and a 5% withdrawal per year out of my 401k, we will be able to retire in 5 years when I turn 60!"

Jane responded, "That sounds wonderful, but how can you be so sure? Do we know your 401k will last?"

Dick put his hand on Jane's. "Absolutely. The numbers show that even if my 401k doesn't earn anything, it wouldn't run out for 20 years!"

"Well, I guess that sounds pretty good," said Jane.

Just then, a large cloud of smoke appeared in their den! Dick and Jane heard the loud sound of an older woman laughing. It almost sounded like cackling! As the smoke faded away, they saw the woman…and couldn't have been more shocked! She was definitely older than they were, was wearing a regal looking long red robe, a crown, and most alarmingly a long scepter with a nasty looking snake wrapped around it. "Who in the world are you?" Dick demanded.

The woman replied, "I am Lady Longevity! My goal is to have as many retirees as possible underestimate how long they will live and ultimately run completely out of money! I am here because I heard your retirement plans, and I have great news! Well, I have great news for **me**. You see, your plan has an excellent chance of failing!"

"Failing? What do you mean?" asked Dick in a panicked tone.

Lady Longevity smiled. "Oh dear. You really have no idea, do you? Let me be blunt. Failure means broke. If you live too long, you run out of money. You don't have enough to pay your bills. You know how people joke about not wanting to eat cat food during their retirement? My goal is to make sure you *have to*!"

Dick and Jane looked at each other. They were dazed and confused. Jane finally broke the awkward silence. "We don't want to go broke. Is this really such a big risk?"

Lady Longevity laughed while pulling out a chair from behind Dick's desk. "Yes, it's a big problem. Do you need me to break it down for you?"

Dick and Jane gulped and nodded, so Lady Longevity began her explanation.

"Look, most people can picture themselves growing old, relatively healthy, enjoying time with loved ones. Well this is a problem, and it goes from the beginning of retirement to the end. People are retiring earlier and they're living longer. It doesn't take a math wiz to realize that means we need to cover more income in between!

We all know we're living longer on average these days, but the *amount* of the increase is amazing: life expectancy in America in 2006 was 77.6 years, while it was only 47.3 years in 1900."[1]

"Wow!" Jane exclaimed, "That's a staggering difference!"

"Absolutely," Lady Longevity continued, "In fact, one study concluded that from 1960 to the year 2000, the average life expectancy increased by seven years, 3.5 of which can be attributable to improvements in health care.[2]

According to the Bureau of Labor Statistics, a healthy couple in their mid-60s have a 50% chance that one spouse will live beyond his or her 91st birthday.[3] That means that this couple has a 50% chance of needing at least 26 years worth of income – and of course it could be many more years than that!

For his book *The Retirement Myth*, author Craig S. Karpel interviewed Robert N. Butler, M.D. on the subject of longevity. Karpel wrote:

> *"Robert N. Butler, M.D. is one of the world's most distinguished authorities on human aging. His 1975 book Why Survive?, exposing what he called "the tragedy of old age in America," won the Pulitzer Prize. "The longevity revolution is one of civilization's most extraordinary achievements. People are generally underestimating the number of years they're going to live, and what those additional years are going to cost them financially. The result is that they're underfunding their old age.""*

Dr. Butler points out that living longer creates two separate problems: not only do we have to generate income for a longer period that many expect, but those years could be some of the most expensive of our entire lives."

Dick sighed. "I guess I didn't plan for all that. It's kind of depressing."

"Alright!" Lady Longevity said proudly, "It's always my goal to make people depressed – you just made my day!"

Dick went from 'kind of depressed' to angry. "The feeling is definitely NOT mutual!"

This made Lady Longevity smile even more, so she asked, "May I continue?" Dick and Jane nodded.

"And of course most wish to retire earlier and earlier," Lady Longevity continued, "As recently as World War II, the average retirement age was 70. Now it's 62.[4]

The worst reality of all here is that early retirement is not always by choice. Whether forced early retirement is due to health reasons or downsizing, the unexpected effect on a retirement plan can be devastating.

In fact, according to Dallas Salisbury of the Employee Benefit Research Institute, 45 percent of Americans retire sooner than they had planned – half of those because of illness or disability.

In 2003, AARP surveyed Americans between the ages of 50 and 70, asking them if they expected to work past normal retirement age. Interestingly, 68 percent said yes, but the most common reason given was financial need.[5]

Gregory Salisbury, Ph.D. sums up this problem perfectly in his book *'But What If I Live?"*

> *"A large portion of these people will be making an erroneous, and perhaps dangerous, assumption. Americans are suffering a common misperception that they will select their own schedule for retirement. … But the reality is that two out of every five Americans won't have a choice of when they retire, because of health issues or job changes."*

So not only are we living longer, but we often stop earning income early – whether it is planned or not!"

Lady Longevity paused here for effect. "Have you ever had a life insurance agent give you a sales pitch?"

Dick sarcastically replied, "Unfortunately."

Lady Longevity ignored his comment and continued with her final point, "At some point, he will most likely ask you a question such as, "What if something happens to you?" Now that we are living so much longer, the smart question to ask is, "What if something DOESN'T happen to you?"

At that moment, Lady Longevity knew her work was done. She had sufficiently depressed both Dick and Jane. So with a swift wave of her wand, a puff of smoke engulfed her and she disappeared.

Dick and Jane stared at each other dumbfounded. All Jane could muster was, "What do we do now?"

Dick hemmed and hawed. "WELL?" Jane demanded.

"Weeellll…" Dick finally admitted, "Remember when Tommy from work retired a few years ago?" Jane nodded yes. "Well, he told me that he never would have tried retiring without the help of a superhero. He said there are seven different retirement villains that would try to ruin your retirement. He thought the only way to protect yourself from them was with a superhero."

"Why in the world did you never share this with me?" Jane demanded.

"Honey, when you hear the superhero's name, I know you're going to agree with me – it sounds ridiculous!" Dick said in a desperate attempt to defend himself.

"Dick, you listen and you listen good," Jane was ready to get on a roll! "You and I know that Metropolis is filled with villains and superheroes. If there are seven different villains that are going to try to sabotage our retirement, you've got to be out of your mind to ignore the help of a superhero, and I don't care HOW silly his name is! So what is it?"

"SuperRetirementPlanner," Dick finally said.

"SuperRetirementPlanner?" Jane asked? Dick nodded yes. "I admit this is a pretty lame name, but regardless, we obviously need his help! You know what that means."

Dick knew immediately: "We need to go talk to Tommy!"

END NOTES

1. Jay Palmer, "Live to 150," Barron's , April 17, 2006
2. Centers for Medicare and Medicaid Services, Office of the Actuary, National Health Statistics Group
3. www.NewYorkLife.com
4. "Beyond 50: A Report to the Nation on Economic Security." AARP 2002
5. Catherine Saillant, "A New Wrinkle in the Workforce," Los Angeles Times, February 24, 2005

Chapter 3

The Invisible Enemy

"IT'S CALLED INFLATION"

Dick's friend Tommy lived nearby. He was relaxing in a rocking chair on his front porch when Dick and Jane pulled into his driveway. They drove in so fast that the screech of the tires almost made Tommy drop the lemonade he had been savoring.

"Dick, is that you?" Tommy asked as his old friend jumped out of his car.

"Yes, it is! Please tell me you have time to talk to us right now!" Dick exclaimed as he and Jane hustled to the front stoop.

Tommy smiled. "Sure. Brenda is spending the afternoon with the grandkids, so I've got nothing but time. You guys look like you've seen a ghost!"

Jane opened her mouth to answer, but Dick beat her to it, "I think we just did – a crazy old lady with a wand and smoke just gave us the strangest and scariest talk of our lives right in the middle of our kitchen – and then she disappeared!"

Tommy couldn't hide his smile. "Let's see…crazy old lady…holding a wand…disappeared in a cloud of smoke…that sure sounds like Lady Longevity."

This time Jane was faster than Dick, "Yes, that's right! How did you know?"

"Jane, I'm so happy you're here," Tommy started. "I know because I retired a few years ago. I've met Lady Longevity. I've also met SIX other retirement villains in short order. Scared the life out of me I don't mind telling you!"

"But why didn't you tell us about all this back then?!" Jane demanded.

Tommy wasn't surprised at all to hear her say that. "Jane, the reason I'm so happy to see you is because I DID tell Dick. He refused to believe me. He said he thought he could figure it all out on his own. But the fact that Lady Longevity paid you a visit tells me your plan isn't complete yet – in fact – it means your plan has a good chance of failing."

Jane was getting more and more upset the more she heard. "That's exactly what Lady Longevity said! Tommy I don't want to be broke in retirement. Is your retirement going alright? How do we make sure ours is safe and secure? Please help us!"

Tommy wanted to calm Jane down, so he moved towards her. He was able to stay calm, as this wasn't the first time friends of his had approached him after being introduced to one or more of the retirement villains. "Jane, please settle down. Let me answer those questions one at a time. My retirement is going wonderfully. Brenda and I couldn't be happier. It's funny really. When we met the retirement villains, we were terrified. But now we're so confident we sleep like happy babies!"

Jane had to jump in, "THAT'S what we want! How do you do that?!"

"I'll tell you exactly what I was taught: before you can solve the problem, you have to identify it, "Tommy explained. "So tell me, how many of the retirement villains have you met so far?"

Dick and Jane could quickly see where this was going. "Just Lady Longevity – just now," Dick said.

"The path to a retirement without worry begins with meeting the other six retirement villains. Unfortunately, you two already look like you've had more than you could handle today." Tommy knew they would want to learn more as soon as possible, but he wanted to hear them say it.

"No!" Dick and Jane exclaimed – and Dick continued, "We're ready for answers – no matter how painful they might be." Jane nodded her agreement.

"Great!" Tommy responded, "That's what I needed to hear. Did you bring your retirement plans and notes with you?" Dick nodded yes and handed Tommy a manila folder. "Perfect, then we can get you on your way. Let's sit down at the dining room table."

The three of them sat down at the table. Dick and Jane sat next to each other – they had to because Dick was holding Jane's hand tightly and wasn't going to let go. He could sense they were about to go on the ride of their lives.

Tommy opened their folder on the table and then looked up. "Okay, I've helped quite a few friends through this process, and I think I know the most logical order to go in. Is it alright if I lead the way?" Dick and Jane quickly agreed. "Good. Let's look at your notes. I see that your income plan gives you the same amount of income every year in your retirement, is that right?"

Dick knew what Tommy was suggesting and immediately jumped into defending himself. "Yes, I did that intentionally. I know things could get more expensive during our retirement, but I figured as we get older, we won't be as active and so we won't be spending as much money each year. So, yeah, the income plan is the same amount each year."

Just then a cloud of smoke appeared near the table. Dick and Jane shouldn't have been surprised, but they were. They both jumped out of their seats a little. But then they settled in and remembered why they were there. Once the smoke cleared, they assumed they would see someone. Except this time, they didn't.

"I don't get it!" Dick bellowed, "I thought we'd see the next retirement villain."

Tommy smiled. "You're going to meet the next retirement villain, but you're not going to see him! You see, he is rarely seen, and I have no doubt he will keep you from seeing him today." Naturally, Dick and Jane couldn't have been more confused!

Just then, the empty chair at the end of the dining table moved slowly away from the table and then stopped. Tommy said, "Hello Invisible Enemy, I was expecting you."

"I know some people weren't expecting me!" A voice came from the chair. Dick and Jane were frozen. At first Tommy laughed. Then he began to lose his patience with their new guest.

"Would you please introduce yourself? Do you really enjoy scaring people that much?" Tommy asked.

"One of my favorite things in the world!" The Invisible Enemy responded! "Hi Dick and Jane, my name is the Invisible Enemy, and I'm here because your retirement plan could lead you to failure. Of course, that's exactly what I WANT to happen!"

Dick looked at Jane and said, "I can't believe I'm about to talk to an empty chair!" Then Dick turned to the chair. "Okay Invisible Enemy, we're here because we trust our friend Tommy, and we're ready to hear the truth. Please explain our problem."

The retirement villain looked over at Tommy who was nodding in agreement. "Very well," he said, "here's your problem. The Invisible Enemy is all around you. NO ONE escapes it. It doesn't just affect retirees, but EVERY single American;

So if I affects everyone and am all around you, why am I so commonly ignored? Because I'm sneaky! Most people don't notice me until it's too late to plan for!

So what is the Invisible Enemy? I'm inflation. Another way of saying it is: things you have to buy go up in price over a period of time.

Does anyone escape inflation? Absolutely not! I wipe out your purchasing power at any income level. I am definitely a non-discriminating villain!

And I am most certainly a terrifying villain when combined with longer lives! Back around the time when Social Security was established, it wouldn't have been unusual for someone to retire at 65 and pass away before they reached the age of 70. Inflation in retirement wasn't a problem.

But how about someone who retires at 62 and passes away at 92? That's a WHOLE different situation isn't it? How about a super quick example to show how this works:

Let's say this 62 year old needs $50,000 per year to live on today. And for the sake of this example, let's say inflation grows during their retirement at exactly 4.8% per year each year.

By the time our retiree passes away at 92, to keep her spending the same would require her income to be *$200,000 a year!* That's a big deal!

And that's why you CAN'T skip the topic of inflation. The Invisible Enemy must be identified and dealt with!

So you might think this would be a big concern to a lot of people. That's definitely not the case! Many people SuperRetirementPlanner meets with have no plan for it and aren't worried about it. Most of their previous advisors never even addressed it.

There's good reason that Bill Staton, CFA, chairman of Staton Financial Advisors, who has managed money for 40 years, said in his September 2009 private client letter:

> *"Whatever you do with your investments, put much higher inflation at the top of your list of obstacles to overcome."*

I'm sure Lady Longevity quoted Dr. Gregory Salsbury, Ph.D.'s book, *But What If I Live?* Here's another great one:

> *"If you forget about inflation altogether, its effect on your retirement lifestyle can be catastrophic. And yet very few people ever stop to consider the severity of inflation's impact."*

Can you guess why so many ignore inflation? Because inflation is The Invisible Enemy. I hope you're catching the theme here!" Dick and Jane nodded yes emphatically.

"So let's look at just how bad inflation typically is." The Invisible Enemy continued, "Since 1914, inflation, as measured by the CPI averaged 3.38 percent per year.[1] But does CPI really tell us how much prices are increasing? Hardly.

There's a very important aspect of inflation that must be discussed. This is about the government and how the government relays information about inflation. You see, most people depend on and turn to the government for information about inflation. Over the past 100 years or so, the government has created indices that it reports every month. These reports tell you how fast prices are going up.

Back in 1913, the government developed a measure of inflation called the Consumer Price Index (CPI) which is a formula that tells the public how high prices have gone up on average over a month's period of time. It's then converted to an annual rate of inflation. For example, the government might say that this month the CPI went up 0.4% (4/10 of 1%), which translates to an annual rate of inflation of approximately 4.8%.

Now, what's the problem with the CPI? First of all, the government uses only a limited number of items in calculating the CPI. This means that the result doesn't necessarily reflect the reality of what you're facing when you buy things on a daily or regular basis.

For example, our government report might report that there is NO inflation. Therefore, Social Security benefits won't be increased. Yet you can't help but notice that during the year your groceries cost 10 to 20% more than the previous year, and depending on the day you're paying 25 to 50% more at the gas pump! That's not what NO INFLATION is supposed to feel like!

Another problem with the CPI is that because it is based on a formula that was developed years ago, it doesn't necessarily mean the formula is correct, nor does it take into account all the variables faced today. Because so many things revolve around how the government reports inflation to you, this can cause serious problems.

Jeffrey A. Hirsch says it well in his 2011 book *Super Boom:*

> *"The U.S. Department of Labor's Bureau of Labor Statistics (BLS) has tweaked and manipulated the Consumer Price Index (CPI) so many times over the past 30 years or so in an attempt to mask inflation that the indicator may very well not detect a true upsurge in inflation in the years ahead."*

According to the U.S. Department of Labor, Bureau of Labor Statistics, since 1965, inflation has averaged 4.78% per year. That's what Uncle Sam says. But is that how our spending power has been affected?

If you want to talk about a difference between what Uncle Sam says, and what reality says, let's see how nursing home costs have risen. In 1964, the monthly cost of a top end, high quality nursing home was about $250 a month. Yes, you heard me correctly!

$250 a month in 1964. Over $5,400 a month in 2011 in Metropolis. By the way, costs are about the same here as in the Columbia, South Carolina area. In some urban areas, the costs top out at over $13,000 a month![2]

How about gasoline? Remember when gasoline was only 29 cents a gallon? Today (2011) it costs $3.66 a gallon.

I could go on making examples all day long, but I think you get the point: what the government tells you about inflation and what it really is are two different things.

In fact, they are so different that many feel that CPI is pretty much a meaningless piece of information. The numbers don't lie. Whatever they are, they are. If the government wants to attempt to soften up this problem, that's its choice. But you know that whatever it costs to buy things is what it costs.

Just how badly do the government numbers miss the mark on inflation? Look at these quotes in the Yahoo Finance article from Tuesday, April 12th, 2011: Inflation Actually Near 10% Using Older Measure

> *"After former Federal Reserve Chairman Paul Volcker was appointed in 1979, the consumer price index surged into the double digits, causing the now revered Fed Chief to double the benchmark interest rate in order to break the back of inflation. Using the methodology in place at that time puts the CPA back near those levels.*

Inflation, using the reporting methodologies in place before 1980, hit an annual rate of 9.6 percent in February, according to the Shadow Government Statistics newsletter.

Since 1980, the Bureau of Labor Statistics has changed the way it calculates the CPI.

Still, going by recent strong comments from Federal Reserve officials, even members of the central bank must believe inflation is being underreported."

10% inflation?! How many people have a plan in place that would protect them from an extended period of time with 10% inflation? Very, very few. Good news for the Invisible Enemy!" Dick, Jane and Tommy all shook their heads.

The Invisible Enemy had one final point he wanted to sink in. "The bottom line is that there is more inflation than you realize. If you don't plan for it, your retirement plan isn't going to work."

Dick had a worried look on his face and sighed. "I think I'm starting to see how I had this wrong."

An Invisible Enemy Example:

Tommy then said, "Go ahead and give them an example."

"Very well," the Invisible Enemy replied. "Grandma Margaret was a retiree in 1965. When her husband passed away he left her with a relatively modest pension from the railroad, a Social Security retirement benefit, and an almost-paid-for home.

In 1965 when she retired, she was receiving a little over $400 a month. She had about $15,000 in the bank, and a mortgage payment of only $97 a month. Her other fixed expenses such as food, utilities, insurance, health costs, etc. only ran about $175-200 a month.

When she retired, Grandma Margaret actually had a small surplus cash flow each month (around an extra $50 a month), money in the bank, and a very secure and peaceful retirement in front of her. Or so she thought!

But over time things really changed. Grandma Margaret was in great health, and ten years after her retirement at age 75, she still had basically the same $400 a month coming in, but her expenses had increased to the point where she was spending more than her income each month.

But she was able to just barely make it. She moved into a retirement home. (She refused to sell her home as all the kids had grown up there and she wanted it stay in the family.) Her monthly expenses were up to around $700 per month. This negative $300 per month in cash flow didn't seem too bad since she had funds in her bank account to cover the shortfall.

Now we move ahead ten years to 1985. Grandma Margaret is 85, still in really good health, and in financial trouble. Her bank accounts are at zero. She's living in the retirement home, still in decent health but failing, and having to depend on the grandkids to put in money each month to pay her bills and take care of her.

If she needed anything, the family had to buy it for her. The $400 a month she was getting at age 65, which seemed OK at the time, was nowhere near enough at age 85!!

Grandma Margaret committed the sin of enjoying good health, and believing that she would be okay in retirement. In fact, The Invisible Enemy inflation had wiped her out."

Over the last few moments, Jane actually let out an audible gasp. Even though this retirement villain was invisible, she was seeing it clearly for the first time; and she was scared. She could see herself in Grandma Margaret's shoes. The Invisible Enemy continued:

"See, Grandma Margaret didn't realize how bad things were, because she was living her life day-by-day and didn't see the jumps in prices all at once. For example, as of right now, gas is $3.66 a gallon. In 1971, if you had told someone that wasn't very familiar with inflation that gas would run $3.66 a gallon, they would have thought it would be too expensive to drive a car.

If you had told that same person in 1968 that his or her $20,100 house would be selling for $138,900 today, they would have thought you were crazy! Heck, in some places, that $20,100 house now sells for more than $300,000!

That $3.66 gallon of gas we bought today, based on an inflation figure of 5% per year, will cost us $5.96 in ten years, and $9.71 in twenty years. Imagine it costing $200 to fill up your car!

The car that you bought for $20,000 with a monthly payment of $310 might cost $30,000 with a monthly payment of $450, ten years from now, and more than double that in twenty years. Can you imagine paying $850 per month for a car payment, just to get an average, nothing-fancy type of car?

Well, it's no easier for you to accept paying that high of a monthly car payment than it was for Grandma Margaret to accept that her $97 month mortgage payment would turn into a $700 month fee at the retirement center for her to have a place to live.

It was no easier for Grandma Margaret to believe that a doctor's visit would cost $125, or that a gallon of milk would be $3.90! The prices we live with and accept as "normal" would have made

Grandma Margaret think you were loony-tunes if you told her what things would cost.

She wouldn't have been able to understand how anyone could survive with prices like that, and as it happened, she didn't survive financially. She lived in her 1965 mentality.

You had better stop thinking those things aren't possible because they will become a reality. Slowly and surely your budget will increase."

Dick had heard enough. "So, what do we do? How do we deal with inflation?" Dick asked.

Although no one in the room could actually see him, The Invisible Enemy had a huge smile on his face. "As far as I'm concerned, DON'T!"

Tommy, however, knew that the Invisible Enemy had provided everything he needed for Dick and Jane's lesson. "Thank you Invisible Enemy. Dick, Jane and I are now going to make a plan to protect them from inflation…from YOU!"

"I refuse to sit around and watch THAT!" A cloud of smoke appeared and there was now quiet at his end of the table.

"I hate to assume," said Jane, "but it appears the Invisible Enemy has left."

Tommy laughed. "Yeah, I guess he could be tricking us; but honestly, I know he was telling the truth. He couldn't bear to watch us set up a plan to protect you from him."

Dick was too worried to laugh. "So I know I've already asked, but how DO we protect ourselves from him?"

"It's actually very easy," Tommy responded. "SuperRetirementPlanner."

Dick looked dejected. Jane jumped in, "Oh, yeah, you mean the guy who can protect us from Lady Longevity too, right?"

"Yes!" Tommy exclaimed, "So Dick DID tell you about him?!"

"Oh yeah, he told me about him alright," an exasperated Jane said. "He told me about him right before I told him to get our butts over to YOUR house!"

Tommy let out a big laugh. He had seen this before. One spouse didn't let the other spouse in on the situation until they absolutely had to. "You came here and asked me how you can protect your retirement from these retirement villains. Well, SuperRetirementPlanner is the way. You asked how Brenda and I have such a peaceful retirement. SuperRetirementPlanner is the reason why. A good retirement planner can be your superhero and help protect you from these villains. You really don't need to know any more than that. But I suppose you might like to know a little about how he's going to do that, wouldn't you?"

Dick and Jane nodded emphatically.

"Okay, here is a *really* quick and simple summary of what he did for me and what he'll do for you. First, he makes sure you realize that you NEED a plan for inflation."

Dick interrupted, "After some quality time with that invisible dude, that is NOT a problem!"

Tommy smiled. "I figured as much. The next thing he's going to do is have you is figure out what your monthly budget is in today's dollars, and come up with a realistic number of how much after-tax income you need to live on today, right now."

Dick jumped in – again! "Okay I admit that I really screwed up this retirement plan, but at least I have that part figured out!"

"Good!" Tommy said. He figured Dick had taken enough abuse for now and could use some encouragement. "Then he will help you estimate how much income you will need and want in retirement. Since you're not yet retired, this can be quite a challenge, but even if you're taking a wild guess, it's a valuable process to go through.

You have to pick one or more inflation rates, and see how much this same monthly budget will cost in the future so you can have the same exact lifestyle throughout your retirement - and MOST importantly protect you from running out of money!

By this point, you can see a great estimate of what type of income you will need each year throughout your retirement. You can then compare these numbers with how much monthly income you expect to receive from sources like Social Security and any pensions. Most likely there will be a difference, and that is what you'll have to cover with your nest egg.

Generating that income from your nest egg is FAR more complicated AND important than most realize, and we'll get to that when we visit with another villain."

"There are still five more, right?" Jane asked.

Tommy was glad Dick and Jane were paying close attention. "That's right – and they're all important. So I think we've covered The Invisible Enemy enough for now. We should really move to the next villain when you two think you're ready. Just never forget, people live a lot longer now which makes the effects of inflation even worse. The longer you live, the more time there is for inflation to eat into your savings!

The only real answer is to plan. Monitor your plan, update your plan and make adjustments as necessary so you're always on target and you don't ever end up like Grandma Margaret."

Dick and Jane looked at each other. Then Dick said, "Don't worry, we definitely don't want that either. And I'm sure I speak for Jane when I say, we want to keep meeting these villains as soon as possible!" Jane nodded in agreement.

"Great," said Tommy, "Then let's keep rolling!"

END NOTES

1. www.tradingeconomics.com/united-states/inflation-cpi
2. www.Genworth.com/content/products/long_term_care/long_term_care/cost_of_care.ht

Chapter 4

Taxes: The Good, the Bad, and the Ugly!

"The hardest thing in the world to understand is the income tax."

Albert Einstein

"Okay, so we've talked to Lady Longevity and the Invisible Enemy. Who's next?" Jane was now on a mission and wanted to find out what else her and Dick needed to know.

Tommy smiled. "Alrighty. Dick, I'm looking at your retirement plan, and you don't really have any information here on taxes. Did you give that much thought?"

"Not really," Dick replied, "I figured taxes are taxes so they wouldn't be much different when we retire."

As soon as he finished his sentence, a large cloud of smoke appeared. Dick and Jane were briefly startled, but as you might imagine, they were starting to get used to this type of thing. Once the dust settled, Dick and Jane saw that there was an old, wrinkled man with white hair and a long beard standing across the room from them. He wore a blue and white striped blazer, bright red pants, a large, red, white, and blue top hat, and he had a crazed look in his eyes.

"I WANT YOU!" He said as he lurched forward and pointed his boney finger at Dick and Jane. This was the first time any of the villains had physically approached them, so they naturally jumped back.

"Want us to *what*?" Dick asked the man as clearly as he could muster.

Tommy knew he needed to introduce everyone. "Dick and Jane, I'd like you to meet the next retirement villain. Please say hello to Evil Uncle Sam."

Before Dick or Jane could say anything, Evil Uncle Sam said, "You know I hate it when you call me evil. Why can't you just call me Uncle Sam?"

Tommy wasn't going to let him play the sympathy card. "Knock it off Sam. You're as evil as they come! You don't want Dick and Jane. You just want their money – and lots of it!" Tommy turned his attention to Dick and Jane. "Guys, uncle Sam used to only stand for good. But Evil Uncle Sam represents everything that is wrong with our government and their spending. Since they can't and won't control their spending, they have to tax us at every possible turn. That's what this man represents."

Evil Uncle Sam didn't say a word, so Dick spoke up: "Okay, so we obviously have to pay income taxes during retirement. Is that all this is about?"

Tommy sadly shook his head. "Oh if it were only that simple. Evil Uncle Sam, it's time for you to give them the truth. Tell Dick and Jane about taxes during retirement; and don't leave anything out. Tell them the good, the bad, AND the ugly."

Evil Uncle Sam gulped. "Everything?" He asked hestiantly. Dick, Jane and Tommy all nodded their heads yes. "Okay," Evil Uncle Sam started, "First of all, I hate to admit it, but taxes are an even bigger deal than most Americans realize. Did you know that taxes are the average American's largest expense? In fact, it's almost twice as much as the second highest category, which is housing. In 2010, combined federal, state and local taxes made up 27.7% of the average American's income."[1]

"That's ugly," Dick interjected.

"Well, I do have to tell the truth," Evil Uncle Sam replied. "And that's just the bad. Here's the ugly: It's quite possible that this is more important than at any other time in our country's history. Just ask anyone if they think tax rates will go up or down in the future. With our government racking up massive deficits year in and year out, most find it hard to imagine a way to avoid tax increases."

As he made this point, Evil Uncle Sam pulled out some slides from the inside breast pocket of his jacket.

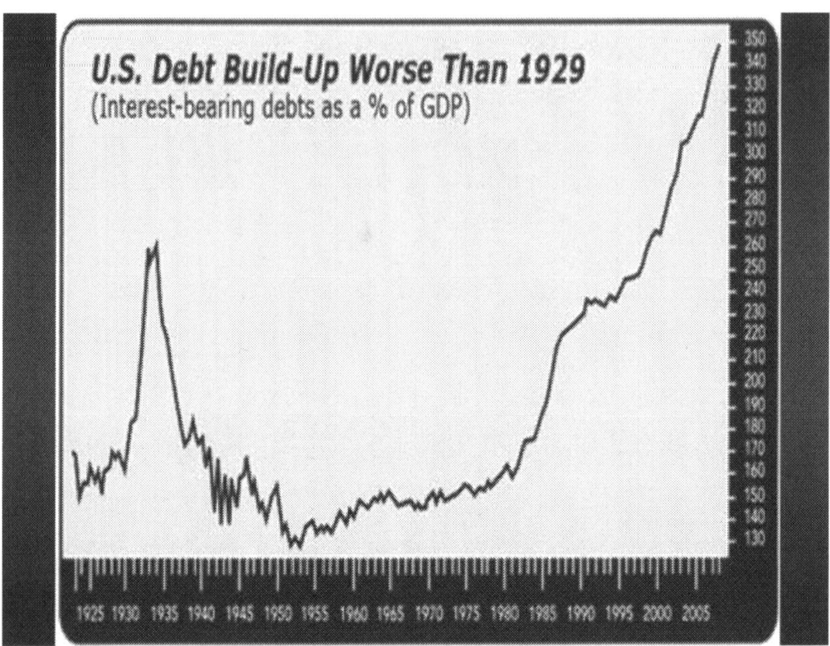

Figure 4.1[2]

"You brought visual aids?" Jane couldn't resist asking.

"I make him bring them because I think people learn much easier that way." Tommy said with a smile.

Evil Uncle Sam rolled his eyes. "Take a look at Figure 4.1. Want another reason to fear higher income taxes in the future? The truth is, while we pay massive amounts of taxes in all areas of our lives, the income tax has been much worse at different times over the last one hundred years. Check out Figure 4.2.

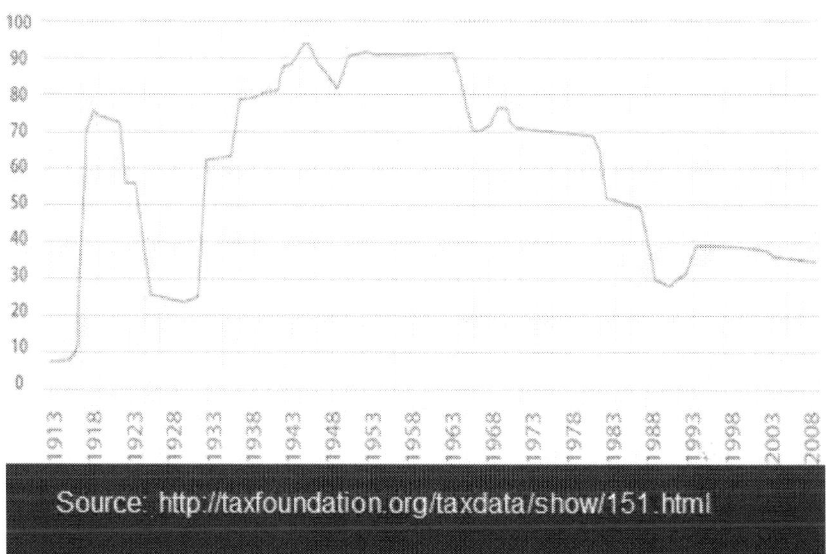

Figure 4.2

As you can see, the highest income tax rates have been MUCH higher than they are right now. So there is clearly a historical precedent. The bottom line is that the government is spending out of control, and it's hard to find any financial advisor who doesn't think taxes are going up. So what does that mean for you? It means you need to plan to lower your taxes now AND attempt to lower them in the future!"

This was music to Dick's ears. "I promise you I am ALL for that!"

Evil Uncle Sam continued, "You should realize that what you do in one area of your financial life will affect all the others. Nowhere is this more true than with taxes. I can't think of a single thing you can do, financially speaking, that does not have an effect on your taxes.

- If you keep your money in the bank, that affects your taxes.

- If you take your money out of the bank and put it somewhere else, that affects your taxes.
- If you sell stocks, that affects your taxes.
- If you buy or sell a house, that affects your taxes.
- If you set up certain trusts and wills for your estate, that affects your taxes.
- If you make gifts, that affects your taxes.
- If you have a part-time or full-time job, that affects your taxes.
- If you own a business, that affects your taxes.

Every activity, financially-speaking, will be reflected somewhere on those tax forms. Since tax planning and investment planning are so intertwined, they must be done together so every decision you make will be integrated and coordinated with the other areas of your financial life.

Another key point regarding tax planning has to do with tax law changes. They come at us fast and furious! This is yet another important reason to not only have an advisor, but to make sure your advisor stays up on changes. Just because planning you do today is legal and to your advantage, it won't necessarily be that way in the future. Therefore, you should make sure your tax planning is reviewed periodically to make any necessary adjustments."

Tommy sensed Evil Uncle Sam stopping. "If that all makes sense, I'm going to have Sam explain a couple of his nasty tax traps to you, and I'll teach you some of the basics of how to avoid those traps that I've learned from SuperRetirementPlanner!"

Jane scribbled her pen on her note pad to make sure there was plenty of ink for notes. Dick, happy to let Jane do all the note taking, leaned back with a huge smile. "Music to my ears!"

Part 1: Avoid Overpaying Income Taxes in Retirement and Taxes on Social Security Benefits

Evil Uncle Sam hated Tommy's attempts to help people, but he couldn't resist sharing the gory details of his tax traps so he started right away, "One of the biggest mistakes retirees make is overpaying income taxes, which includes the additional income taxes caused by Social Security income. It's been said that it's like there are two different tax codes in America: There is one while you're working and there is a completely different one when you are retired. Your Social Security benefits being taxed is definitely one of the driving reasons for such a comment.

Let's start at the beginning. FDR established Social Security in 1934, and there was a promise that it would never be taxed. Sadly politicians paid no attention to that promise…"

"BIG surprise!" Dick couldn't help interrupting.

Evil Uncle Sam rolled his eyes again. He hated that part of his talk because it always seemed like someone interrupted! He continued, "1983 is when Social Security benefits were first taxed. Then the amount of your Social Security benefits that could be taxed was increased in 1993, and now up to 85% of your Social Security Benefits may be subject to tax.

Now, Social Security and its problems have been in the news a lot the last few years, and one of the solutions to help fund future Social Security payments that is often discussed is increased taxation of benefits. Back in 2005, AARP presented their 9 ways to fix Social Security without privatization, and the #3 topic there was to raise taxation on benefits.[3] Some have called the taxation of Social Security benefits a "tax on the wealthy," yet about 40% of recipients are currently affected.[4] So this costs almost half of current recipients, and that's WITHOUT increased taxation."

Dick was mad. "Tax on the wealthy my…" he started but Jane wouldn't let him finish. "Uh, honey, you're right. That's clearly not fair. Let's let him continue." Dick leaned back in his chair. He had a lot he wanted to say, but he bit his tongue.

"Thank you," Evil Uncle Sam said, "So taxation of Social Security benefits costs an awful lot of retirees, and it could get worse. Let's look at how it works and some ways to try and avoid it. Let's start with Don and Joan."

"I hope you like this example," Tommy interjected, "It was my idea. I like examples. Plus the cool part is they are real people and it shows their real situation. They live right here in Metropolis!"

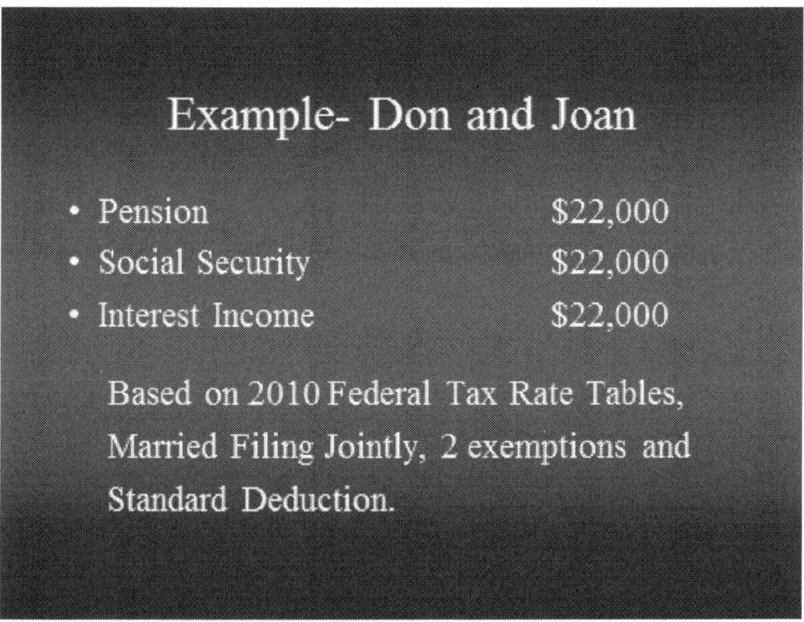

Figure 4.3

Evil Uncle Sam rolled his eyes yet again. "As you can see from Figure 4.3, Don and Joan are comfortably living off of a pension, Social Security and interest income. Please keep in mind everyone has different income in retirement. So whether your income might be higher or lower than theirs, the process still applies.

So Don and Joan are happy with their income but they want to lower their taxes. Have you ever heard the idea that you won't pay much in taxes in retirement?"

Dick and Jane both nodded.

Evil Uncle Sam loved sharing this part. "Well that's certainly not always the case. In federal income taxes alone, Don and Joan are paying almost $6,000 a year; but that's not all. Some find the effect of taxation on their Social Security benefits to be downright shocking: every time they make an additional dollar, they now have to pay taxes twice. Many call this the retiree double tax.

So let me give you a simplified example. Let's say Don and Joan's bank raises their interest rate just a little bit and they make one extra dollar in their savings account this year. Of course when they make an extra dollar they have to pay taxes on it. They are in the 25% tax bracket, so they owe $0.25 cents of income tax on the extra dollar. But their Social Security benefits trigger an additional tax. For Don and Joan, this is another $0.21 cents of tax on the extra dollar.

So Don and Joan made an extra dollar, and they have to give back 46 cents in Federal taxes. At this time the highest tax rate in America is 35%.[4] So even the wealthiest people in the country like Bill Gates and Warren Buffet are paying no more than 35% on taxes. Yet here we have Don and Joan, middle class retirees, paying 46 cents on the dollar on that extra dollar."

Don and Joan Have 2 Tax Problems:

- 1) Total Taxes are $5,907 a Year
- 2) Every Additional Dollar They Bring in is Taxed 2 Times:

25¢ Income Tax

21¢ Tax on Social Security Benefits

= 46¢ Paid in Taxes

Figure 4.4

Dick was downright angry. "Wait a second! All those rich CEO's with the private jets and yachts, and 10 different houses all over the world are maxed out at 35% taxes, and regular retired folks like Don and Joan have to pay as much as 46% in taxes on some of their money?! That's not just unfair. That's criminal!"

Tommy nodded in agreement. "I couldn't agree more. I have no doubt you understand why this process is so important. We have to make sure your plan gives you every chance to avoid this stuff."

"It better!" Dick replied while leaning back and crossing his arms.

Evil Uncle Sam took that as his cue to continue. "It's clearly not fair; and with regard to Don and Joan's Social Security and pensions, there is no planning you can do to change how they affect their Social Security taxation. The only thing we can work with is their income from savings and investments.

Fortunately for me, almost all your savings and investments are going to help trigger this taxation. This includes any kind of bank or credit union accounts like CDs, savings accounts and money markets. If you have a retirement account and you are withdrawing money from it, that is going also contribute to the Social Security taxation.

The same is true of any kind of stock and mutual fund dividends and capital gains. Rental and bond income are included as well. In fact even tax-free bond interest is included!" As he said these things, Evil Uncle Sam for the first time had a smile on his face. In fact, it was a devilish grin.

Tommy had seen this look way too many times. "Hey! You're not here to brag about how you get money out of people – you're here to tell them how this works."

Evil Uncle Sam, you guessed it, rolled his eyes and then said, "Fine then. If you don't like my way of explaining it, YOU do it!"

"I thought you'd never ask!" Tommy said in a huff, "So the only types of investments that can help you avoid this taxation are anything that has some kind of tax deferral to it. Some examples would include

- A retirement account you are not withdrawing from,
- Deferred Annuities
- Some Income Annuities, and
- Savings bonds"

Evil Uncle Sam was visibly irritated. He knew where this was going, and Tommy was happy to press forward, "Do you guys want to see how SuperRetirementPlanner helps so many retirees reduce the taxation on Social Security benefits?"

Dick and Jane both leaned forward. Dick answered first (as usual): "Jane is all ready to take notes!" Now it was Jane's turn to roll her eyes.

Tommy was excited to continue. "He uses an idea called Tax-Advantaged Income. Now, this type of planning looks very different for different people in different situations. You can set it up before you need the money and take it later, or you can set it up and start taking income right away. So it really depends on your personal situation.

Also, to really go into it, we would have to get into all kinds of IRS documents. Because of those reasons, I don't go into the nitty gritty of *how* it works. I'll just show you *what* it does for you. What it boils down to is, the goal is to see if you can reduce or eliminate taxation of Social Security benefits. If he will help you, SuperRetirementPlanner will show you how it would work for you."

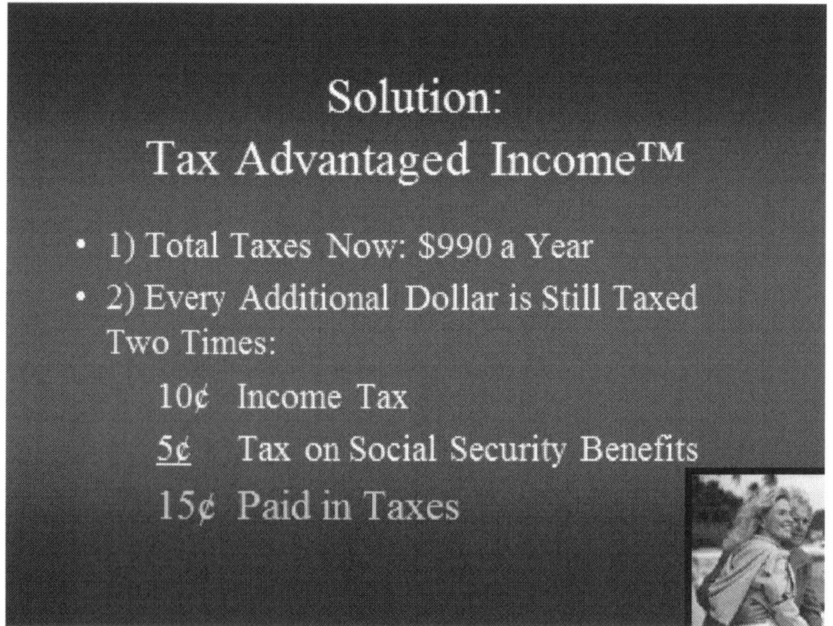

Figure 4.5

So let's look at Don and Joan's situation after they implement their Tax Advantaged Income Plan. Look at Figure 4.5. With Tax-Advantaged Income, Don and Joan's total taxes would drop to about $990 a year."

"Holy cow!" Dick exclaimed, "Weren't they paying almost $6,000 a year before?" Tommy nodded yes. Dick was now getting excited. "That's an unbelievable difference!"

Tommy smiled because he loved teaching this part. "Now in their case, taxes on Social Security benefits weren't eliminated. BUT, they now only pay 10 cents of income tax on an extra dollar made and 5 cents of tax on their Social Security benefits. So if Don and Joan DID earn that one additional dollar of income, they would go from paying 46 cents of tax on that dollar down to 15 cents of tax.

Solution:
Tax Advantaged Income™

• Compare:	Before	After
• Spendable Income	$66,000	$66,000
• Income Taxes:	$5,907	$990
• Amount of Tax on Last Dollar Earned:	46 cents	15 cents

Bottom Line Savings:
$4,917 Every Year

Figure 4.6

In figure 4.6, you can compare their previous and current situations side by side. Their income stayed exactly the same each month. The only difference is they are paying almost $5,000 less in income taxes. And, the thing that excites me about saving on taxes is generally it is going to be an annual savings. So in their case they're saving over $4,900 every single year."

"You're excited!" Dick shouted. "This is probably old hat for you. It's downright thrilling to me!" He said with a huge grin on his face. Jane couldn't resist smiling as well.

Tommy was smiling too. "While our guest is here, we should have him cover one more topic."

"Oh, I don't mind if we skip it," Evil Uncle Sam quickly shot back.

Tommy was not going to have any of his attitude, "Sam, enough with the delays. Get on with the last topic so we can get rid of you."

Part 2: Avoid Forcing Your Loved Ones to Pay Income Taxes Right Away on Your Retirement Accounts

Now it was Evil Uncle Sam's turn to get angry. But he had no choice but to comply and began, "When the Economic Growth and Tax Relief Reconciliation Act (EGTRRA) was signed into law on June 7th of 2001, it affected retirement plans in numerous ways; and that's what this topic is about: your retirement accounts. Any kind of IRAs, 401k, profit sharing, or Teacher and Employee Retention Incentive (TERI) money you might have accumulated. The most important point here is that these types of retirement accounts are handled very differently than any other account you have.

For example, if you have a will, it says who your assets go to when you pass away; One asset your will has no control over is your retirement account. Instead, your retirement accounts are controlled by its beneficiary forms.

Your retirement accounts are also different than other savings vehicles because you're deferring taxes on it as its accumulating. This may be the best way to accumulate money while you are working but of course when you retire and withdraw from the account, you have to pay taxes on all that money.

In addition to paying taxes on your retirement account withdrawals, it can be a very costly way to pass money on to your beneficiaries. This is because they have to pay all the income taxes on it; and it's possible that there might be an estate or inheritance tax on that money as well. That's another double tax right there."

Tommy had heard enough, "Okay Sam. I'll take it from here. So the good news is this 'new' rule that was put into place in 2001. Let's compare it to the old rule. Under the old rules, if you pass a retirement account on to anyone other than your spouse, they would have to pay all the taxes all at once.

The more current rule is usually called a Stretch IRA - you may have heard that term before. The Stretch IRA rule says your beneficiaries can inherit this money and stretch out the taxes on that account over their lifetime. And the thing that is amazing about that, just by avoiding all those taxes in lump sum, there can be a huge tax savings and it can allow that money to continue growing which can be an incredible benefit to your family.

This concept is so valuable, in his 2005 book "Parlay Your IRA into a Family Fortune," IRA guru Ed Slott (widely considered the foremost expert on Stretch IRA's) calls the Stretch IRA:

> *"The Ninth Wonder of the World – the phenomenon I call "compound interest on steroids""*

Now typically with a Stretch IRA, you still maintain full control--so you can invest it however you want, and you can still spend the money however and whenever you want. This is just setting it up correctly in case you don't spend it all. This makes sure that your family doesn't have to pay any unnecessary taxes. So let's take you through this with an example.

Mary is 65. She's got an IRA with $100,000, and we're going to assume she passes away at 83 and at that time her daughter is 40 years old and she has a grandson who is 20. And we are going to assume 6% return here.

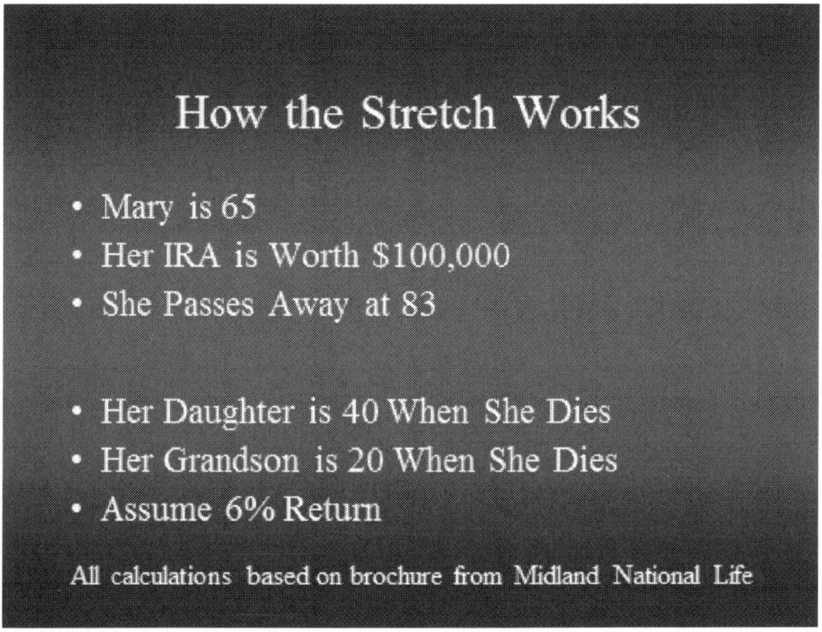

How the Stretch Works

- Mary is 65
- Her IRA is Worth $100,000
- She Passes Away at 83

- Her Daughter is 40 When She Dies
- Her Grandson is 20 When She Dies
- Assume 6% Return

All calculations based on brochure from Midland National Life

Figure 4.7

Now Mary has $100,000, and she is not withdrawing from it right now; but when she turns 70 ½ years old she will have to take some money out every single year – called her required minimum distribution.

Even after all those withdrawals, by the time she passes away she'll have about $220,000 in that account. If it is not set up properly and she passes that onto her family in lump sum, they will have to pay income taxes on the entire $220,000 all at once. Imagine if someone is already in the 25% federal tax bracket or worse. Then add an additional $220,000 to their income. They're going to have to pay a LOT of taxes!"

Jane's jaw dropped. "Wait a second. She leaves $220,000 to her family and they have to pay a huge chunk of it back in taxes?" Tommy sadly shook his head yes while Evil Uncle Sam shook his head yes with a nasty smile. She continued, "Talk about unfair, that's ridiculous."

Tommy nodded in agreement. "Unfortunately that's the system. I think that explains the bad news pretty well. I think we can move to the good news; and if we're going there, we definitely don't need our repulsive guest over here. How does it sound if we get rid of him?"

"With pleasure!" Dick replied with excitement. While answering he got up out of his chair as if he was going to confront Evil Uncle Sam.

"Wait a second! Wait just a second!" Evil Uncle Sam said as he jumped out of his chair and backed away from the table. "I'll go. I promise I'll go. I just have one last thing to say." Tommy groaned in anticipation of what he was about to hear.

Evil Uncle Sam smiled the most sinister smile he could, while rubbing his hands together. He said, "Just remember, I'm here to take as much of your money as I can. Why? Because I loooove to spend money! And don't forget, I have the power to tax you, and you know I will! Hahaha!" His laugh was just as sinister as his smile.

At this, Tommy also jumped out of his chair. That was enough to have Evil Uncle Sam wave his hand in the air. A cloud of smoke appeared and Evil Uncle Sam disappeared.

Tommy went back to his chair and sat down. "I despise that guy." Dick and Jane nodded in agreement and Tommy continued, "Let's focus on the good news now. If Mary sets it up her account as a Stretch IRA and passes it onto her daughter, her daughter can inherit that money and she can take some money out every year and let the rest of it continue to avoid taxes.

And in this example, by the time she passes away she'll have actually taken out over $1,000,000 dollars out of that account. Look at Figure 4.8. Mary's daughter is just taking a portion of the money out every year and she is deferring paying taxes on the balance left in the account.

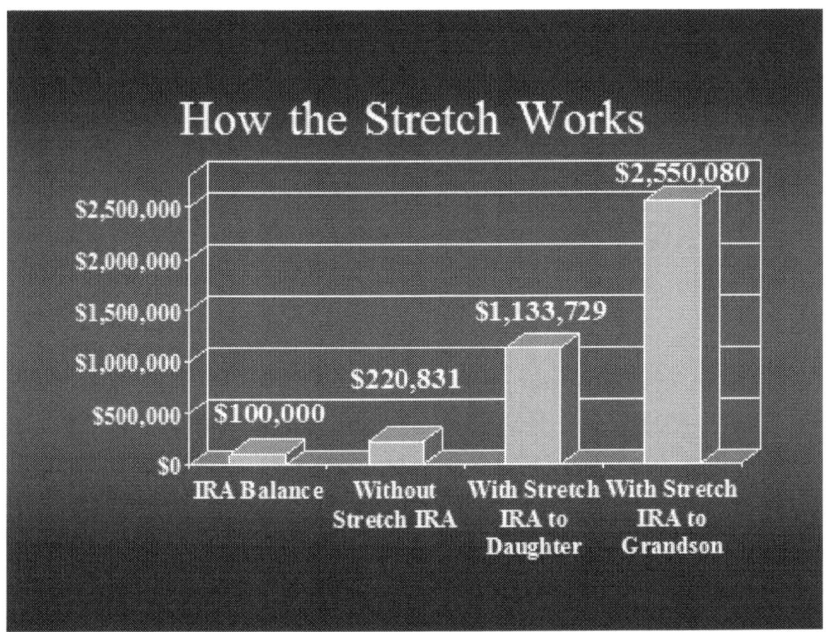

Figure 4.8

If Mary wanted to leave this entire account to her grandson, he obviously has a longer life expectancy so he can spread the taxes out even longer. Over his lifetime he could actually take out over $2,500,000 - all from an account that started with $100,000!

I like to give the example of wealthy families over generations like the Rockefeller's, the Vanderbilt's and the Kennedy's. These types of families have always had special strategies to use like this. But for those of us that don't have that kind of wealth we never had an option to do something so powerful for our family. And, now we do."

Jane was following along and wanted to ensure she understood correctly. "Wow. Okay, so if Mary did nothing using these assumptions, her family would inherit $220,000. Is that part right?" Tommy smiled and nodded yes.

Jane was rolling now. "Alright. Using the Stretch IRA and the assumptions you used, the daughter is able to withdraw over one million dollars over her lifetime, or the grandson would withdraw over two and a half million dollars over his lifetime, right?"

"You've got it exactly Jane!" Tommy was happy to see Jane getting more involved.

"So in this example the choices are $220,000 or at least one million dollars before taxes. That might be the easiest decision anyone could ever make!" Jane summed things up perfectly.

Tommy was happy to have helped Jane understand, and followed up on her thought. "Absolutely. Now, there are different ways to set it up. Mary could leave some of it to her grandson and some to her daughter. She may not want to give her grandson full control over his share. So there are a few things to remember on these kinds of accounts.

First, your investment company or retirement plan must allow it. In 2001 when this law first changed a lot of companies didn't want to mess with the tax reporting so they wouldn't do it. Stretch IRA expert Ed Slott had the following to say *in Parlay Your IRA into a Family Fortune*:

> *"The IRS regulations stipulate that any designated beneficiary can stretch distributions on an inherited IRA over his or her lifetime. Period. Nevertheless, some IRA custodians don't allow the stretch. So while you still have the leverage you should move your money now to an IRA custodian that does. Your beneficiaries may not be able to after you're gone."*

When SuperRetirementPlanner set my accounts up as Stretch IRA's, he made sure the company holding my retirement account would allow the funds to be stretched out to my beneficiaries. In addition to talking to the company, he had to get his hands on the 'fine print.' In my case, it was in something called an IRA Disclosure Statement.

Second, you need to take care of this while you're still alive! I know that sounds silly, but you must know that your beneficiaries can't go back and fix this. As IRA guru Ed Slott says in his book *The Retirement Savings Tax Bomb - and How to Diffuse it*:"

> *"But in order to gain the best possible stretch option, all the pieces have to be put in place by the IRA owner while he or she is still breathing. And if you don't make the right choices now, your beneficiaries will be stuck."*

Tommy continued, "The third thing that SuperRetirementPlanner recommends is not an IRS requirement but can be extremely valuable. It is a Customized Beneficiary Document. Remember when I mentioned that your will doesn't control your retirement accounts? This document does, and every good planner will make sure your retirement account beneficiary documents match up with your wishes.

There are a couple other reasons the Customized Beneficiary Document is so important. First, virtually all company beneficiary forms ask you only one thing: who do you want the money to go to?

This Customized Beneficiary Document can completely personalize how you want everything to be handled by and for your beneficiaries. If you think about it, this is really huge. So many people save so much in their retirement accounts, and since withdrawals are taxable, account holders often withdraw as little as possible from those accounts. So these are some of the most likely assets you'll be leaving to your family. If you're like me you want to make sure they're handled correctly!"

Jane answered, "We're definitely like you. It's scary to think that after you're gone things may not be handled the way you expected."

"Exactly," Tommy agreed, "So what do I mean by personalizing? Let me run through some examples of situations that SuperRetirementPlanner has told me about:

- Are any of the beneficiaries minors? Grandkids maybe? If so, are you *completely* comfortable with them having *total* access to their share at 18 years old? Unless you have set something up to keep this from happening, that is the default; and remember, not only could an 18 year old waste a lot of money, they can do a lot of harm with it too, right?
- Do you have a son-in-law or daughter-in-law that you don't want to leave your money to? This type of document can help keep your hard earned money "in the blood."
- Did you know that if you have multiple children and grandchildren, the typical beneficiary form will disinherit some of the grandchildren in certain situations? This form can eliminate that risk.

- Does your beneficiary having access to all the money at once concern you? This form can help make sure that doesn't happen.

These are just a few of the more common situations SuperRetirementPlanner told me about – and he said there are probably dozens more! So I hope that shows you the power and importance of the Customized Beneficiary Document; and I hope our time with our nasty tax villain has proved to you how vital it is to do planning to keep your taxes as low as possible in retirement!"

Dick and Jane both smiled. "Without a doubt!" Dick responded, "I don't want to give that guy a penny more than I have to!"

"That was just the response I expected," Tommy said. "Look, it's late, and you've had a very long day. I know you probably are eager to hear from the rest of the retirement villains, but let's stop here and pick up bright and early tomorrow."

This time Jane beat Dick to the punch. "I agree. As much as I'd like to do all this in one day, it's just too much. We'll see you tomorrow. At sunrise!"

END NOTES

1. Tax Foundation, Tax Freedom Day and Tax Burden, March 31st, 2011
2. www.marketoracle.co.uk/Article7224.html
3. AARP Bulletin, January 2005, 9 ways to fix Social Security without privatization
4. Social Security: CNBC Explains, www.cnbc.com/id/43840296
5. www.irs.gov/pub/irs-pdf/f1040es.pdf

Chapter 5

The Skyrocketing Cost of Healthcare

"The baby boomers' later life is going to be longer and more expensive than that of any previous generation."

Craig Garber, *The Retirement Myth*

Dick and Jane headed straight home. It had been a long and exhausting day. They drove most of the way in silence. Dick was ashamed and embarrassed. He felt as the man of the house, he should have been able to do all the retirement planning himself.

Finally, he broke the silence, "Honey, I'm so sorry. I figured I could do the whole plan myself. I had absolutely no idea how complicated a retirement plan could be!"

When she had first heard that Dick hadn't shared Tommy's warnings, Jane was furious. But as the day had gone on, she realized that Dick's intentions were good all along. "Darling, that's so sweet of you. I was mad at you before, but I understand that you felt the pressure to provide for us. Not only while you're working, but also in retirement; and I realize that you wanted to get it all right. I really do understand."

Dick was relieved. The last thing he wanted to do was harm his beautiful wife of 36 years.

"But…" she continued, "You DO know how much we need SuperFinancialPlanner now…right?"

Dick quickly nodded. "Believe me honey, I get it. We've only met three of these crazy villains, and yes, I definitely get it!" He smiled at his wife as he pulled into the driveway. After he parked the car, they shared a long embrace. Even with all the bad news shared by the retirement villains, they felt like they actually knew how to put together a successful retirement plan for the first time in their lives. It was a liberating feeling!

That night, Dick and Jane fell fast asleep within seconds of their heads hitting their pillows. It wasn't just the exhaustion of the day – it was also the peaceful feeling of getting on track with their plan. After they'd been sleeping a while, there was a sudden cloud of smoke at the end of the bed. When the smoke cleared, a woman appeared. She wore a nurses uniform, and in her left hand she held a pile of medical bills.

Dick and Jane had never been more startled. They were shocked and disoriented. At the end of the bed stood their guest – she greeted them with a belly laugh.

"Did I surprise you?" She somehow managed to ask as she continued laughing.

"Oh my goodness, you're a retirement villain aren't you?!" Dick exclaimed, "You could have given me a heart attack!"

At this the woman laughed even harder. "That's hilarious, especially considering who I am!"

"So you ARE a retirement villain?" Dick asked, "This is crazy. It's like A Christmas Carol or something! I hope we won't be visited by two more ghosts tonight – at some point I'm going to need some sleep!"

The woman said, "Very funny. But I can assure you that I am NOT a ghost. I am real; and one of the nastiest retirement villains in existence if I do say so myself."

By this time, Dick and Jane had calmed down. They had met 3 other retirement villains just that day. Once the shock of being awoken by a person at the end of the bed had subsided, they realized they were just back on the same ride they were on earlier in the day.

Jane joined the conversation: "Okay we give, who are you?"

"I thought you'd never ask!" The woman responded – with a smile of course. "My name is Sarah Self-Pay. It is such a pleasure to meet you!"

"Sarah Self-Pay?" Dick and Jane said simultaneously and looked at each other. Dick continued, "What in the world does that mean?"

"I am the retirement villain of health care," Sarah Self-Pay responded, "You see, having medical problems is bad enough; but when you have to pay astronomical amounts of money for your healthcare, well that just adds insult to injury. Literally. Get it?" She belly laughed at her own joke.

Jane heard what Sarah Self-Pay was saying, but was still confused. "Okay I guess that makes some sense. But we have health insurance; and when we retire we'll have Medicare, so aren't we pretty much taken care of when it comes to this stuff?"

Sarah Self-Pay began to laugh even harder. "Oh, that's always the funniest thing everyone says! So you have no idea, do you? It sounds to me like I need to give you the whole story. Are you ready?"

Dick and Jane nodded yes. "Ok," Sarah Self-Pay began, "I promise I won't skip a thing – because I just LOVE sharing bad news! Let's see…where to begin. Okay how about here:

For your retirement plan to be effective, it must take into consideration issues that are currently having the greatest financial impact on seniors and retirees. Few would argue that the cost of disability and long-term care is one of the biggest. Some would say it has become the greatest financial threat to middle-class and upper-middle-class Americans today.

In 2001, the National Endowment for Financial Education sponsored a two-day symposium in Scottsdale, Arizona, to study one of the most critical issues faced by retirees. The underlying theme found throughout the report generated from this "think tank" was that long-term care had the potential to become a national crisis.[1] Ten years later we have overwhelming evidence of the problem as more than 12 million Americans need some form of long-term care.[2] In 1950, healthcare costs represented approximately 4% of the average American household budget. By 2004, that percentage has skyrocketed to 17%!"[3]

"Oh my!" Jane interjected, "That's a scary statistic!"

As difficult as it was to imagine, Sarah Self-Pay's smile got even bigger. "Oh don't worry. I've got plenty more bad news!

So what is the cause? As I'm sure Lady Longevity covered with you, Americans are living longer than ever before; and as the population ages, we can expect that the need for long-term care will increase proportionately. The Baby Boomers are aging – the first of 79 million of them will turn 65 this year.[4] And according to US Census projections, over the next 30 years, the number of Americans age 65 will increase by 76 percent. This means that by the year 2030, one in five Americans will be a senior citizen![5] With an aging population facing increased health care needs and rising care costs, and many with no insurance coverage to pay for it, we certainly could have a long-term care crisis of epic proportions.

There wasn't much talk of nursing homes and assisted living facilities back in the '70s. But from 1970 to 1990, nursing home expenditures in the United States increased faster than any other health care cost in this country, with a 12.7 percent annual rate of growth.[6] By 1990, 10.2% of Americans age 75 and older lived in nursing homes.[7]

Another contributing factor to this potential crisis is that medical advancements and improvements in health care now help us survive things like heart attacks and strokes that were more likely to kill us 40 years ago. Medical technology has produced new drugs, diagnostic equipment and cutting-edge surgeries that add years to the average life expectancy of retirees. So an advanced health care system is keeping seniors alive well into their 80's and 90's, often well past their initial projected life expectancy.

The average stay in a nursing home varies, of course, with a person's illness, medical condition and general state of health. The longer we live, the more susceptible we become to other illnesses that typically affect the aged, such as Alzheimer's disease, vascular dementia, and severe mobility problems. Clearly, this increases the demand for nursing homes and assisted living facilities. These conditions, like many that affect the elderly, don't respond well to medications and surgeries, and aren't easily or successfully treated or cured.

Instead, as these illnesses progress, they often lead to a need for custodial care – and lead the aging senior down the path to the poorhouse trying to pay for that care. As the Invisible Enemy should have told you, the average cost of a nursing home stay is $75,000 per year! And these costs have been rising for years. That is a retirement expense that was never contemplated by most seniors, and their financial portfolios could never take that kind of a hit.

Another reason this has become such a big crisis is the geographic expansion of the American family. It wasn't that long ago when most children stayed close to home. Now, instead of moving down the road or across town, many adult children are moving across the state, country, or even overseas. Regardless of whether they're moving by choice or out of need to look for work, this is a game changer for the health care of the family.

When an elderly parent or grandparent became ill, it was easier for children and grandchildren to help with care and keep their disabled family member at home. One by one, families have become separated – spread out across the country – and are no longer as easily able to help when dad has a stroke or mom falls and breaks her hip. This shift in the modern-day family is just one of the many dynamics that has led us to where we are today: with a potential long-term care crisis.

Government programs like Medicare and Medicaid were not initially designed to handle the number of seniors who are in need of care today. And as you will see, Medicare turns its back on seniors in their greatest time of need, and doesn't care about long-term care. Without any help from government or private insurance, how long will it take for your money to run out if you get stuck with a monthly bill of $6,000 or more? How many senior citizens could afford that bill? More and more aging seniors face declining health with rising life expectancy, an increased need for health care and no way to pay for it."

"That is awful!" Jane said. "You said something about Medicare not helping us as much as we expect. What do you mean by that?"

MEDICARE – THE VANISHING GOVERNMENT BENEFIT

"Ah, great question!" Sarah Self-Pay always enjoyed some participation. It let her know she was scaring her listeners – which brought her great joy. "I like to call Medicare the Vanishing Government Benefit! Here's why:

Despite the rapidly increasing need for long-term care services, and the rising costs of those services, most seniors and their families are still shocked to learn that Medicare doesn't pay for nursing home or assisted living costs. They mistakenly believe that Medicare is going to take care of them forever, like it has in the past. Unfortunately, this false sense of security contributes to inaction – the failure to plan ahead – which can be financially devastating when disability strikes. The reality is: Medicare doesn't care about long-term care.

It's easy to see why Medicare and Medicaid will do whatever it takes to avoid paying for your nursing care. The extent of the federal government's long-term liabilities and net commitments to programs such as Medicare and Medicaid is not well known among the general public. These commitments have risen from just over $20 trillion in fiscal 2000 to more than $43 trillion in fiscal 2004.[9]

And just read this from Bloomberg BusinessWeek February 28, 2011:

> *"Let me share one statistic that shocked me, from the Long-Term Budget Outlook published last year by the nonpartisan Congressional Budget Office. If you current trends continue, the CBO says, entitlement spending (Social Security, Medicare and Medicaid) and net interest payments combined will equal all of deferral revenue by 2025, just 14 years from now. Back in 1999, the crossover point was not supposed to happen until 2060."*

Let me give you a picture of how Medicare works with an example:

Joan was beside herself. Steve, her husband of 50 years, had a severe stroke five weeks ago. Steve had been hospitalized for several weeks; first in acute care and then on a skilled floor for rehabilitation. Steve's doctor then released him from the hospital, and he was transferred to a nursing home for additional therapy.

Joan, like so many others, believed that Medicare would cover the cost of his rehabilitation. When someone told her Medicare wouldn't last forever, she still thought it would definitely pay for the first 100 days of therapy. Joan mistakenly assumed that Steve's "one hundred days" started when he entered the nursing home, but that is not accurate. Steve's Medicare days started at the hospital when he began receiving rehabilitation on the skilled floor.

By the time Steve went to the nursing home, he had used some of those Medicare days to pay for the rehabilitation at the hospital. Steve made some progress in physical and speech therapy at the nursing home for a few weeks, but by the third week his progress slows down and then stops. Joan is worried that her husband has become depressed because he is in the nursing home and may have given up; or perhaps his medication is affecting his ability to do the exercises. She feels helpless and doesn't know what to do to get her husband to keep improving.

Steve's physical therapist reports to his doctor, who reports to Medicare, that Steve is no longer showing improvement. Then Joan gets a phone call from the social worker at the nursing home – she has received notice from Medicare, stating that because he is no longer making progress in his therapy, Steve is no longer considered to be rehabilitating; therefore, Medicare is shutting off and will no longer pay his nursing home bill. But wait: What about his "one hundred days?" Well, you don't always get to use those one hundred days, and in Steve's case Medicare abandoned him much earlier. Joan is distraught. How can she afford to pay a $6,000 a month nursing home bill? Where will they get the money? What's going to happen to her husband? What's going to happen to her?

So many people just like Joan and Steve are abandoned by Medicare in their greatest time of need. Because the maximum amount of time Medicare will pay for skilled care is 100 days – but the average number of days actually paid for is much less. Provided the patient has spent three days in the hospital first, and is then transferred to the nursing home from the hospital, Medicare will typically pay 100% of the first 20 days of the patient's stay at a Medicare-certified skilled nursing care facility.[10]

Afterwards, the patient is responsible for a co-pay of roughly $130.00 per day, and Medicare may pay the balance due to the nursing home for an additional 80 days.[10] However, Medicare's continued payment is contingent on the patient receiving rehabilitation and showing improvement with therapy. If you hit a plateau and stop improving, or your therapist and physician determine that no additional rehabilitation is warranted or possible (like a patient with dementia or Alzheimer's Disease), Medicare will shut off with no warning, leaving you scrambling to find alternative forms of payment and jeopardizing your health care in the process.

How is this possible? Why are some people bearing enormous health care costs while others have all their bills paid by Medicare? Because Medicare doesn't cover custodial care if it is the only kind of care you need. Custodial care essentially includes assistance with basic activities of daily living, like walking, transferring, toileting, eating, bathing and grooming.

So when seniors need help getting in and out of bed or walking or bathing; help finding their way to the bathroom or taking their medicine or eating; help remembering how to sit down or drink water; when seniors are at their most vulnerable, and need the most care, our health system often leaves them with few options.

What happened to John F. Kennedy's vision for universal medical insurance for all aged Americans?[11] The Medicare program was supposed to be there for all seniors regardless of their health care needs. Instead, it has shrunk to exclude those afflicted with some of the most devastating illnesses – even though they most likely paid into the Medicare system since its inception.

It doesn't make sense but it's true. If you need heart surgery, chemotherapy, a hip replacement: Medicare pays. If you have Alzheimer's disease, severe dementia, or are completely bedridden:

Medicare does not pay. It's like the diagnosis lottery, where certain illnesses are covered and others are not. How is that fair?"

Dick was furious now. "That's ridiculous! Why in the world would our government favor some illnesses over others?!"

"Yes, that's it exactly!" Sarah Self-Pay responded, "I'm so glad you can see. I've made quite a mess for retirees haven't I? So anyway, the bottom Line is: If you can't get better, Medicare won't help you.

Let's consider many of the different health care situations you could find yourself in; and we'll look at how or if the various government programs will assist you. We start with the healthy, vigorous senior. She may still be working or have recently retired, and is active in family or community life. She may take some medication, and may eventually develop chronic health problems like diabetes or heart disease. She may face hospitalizations or surgeries, and may ultimately have declining health with mobility issues.

Throughout this stage of her health care, Medicare does a really good job of paying many of the bills. Whatever Medicare doesn't cover, supplemental health insurance often makes up the difference.

The following example is a perfect illustration: If you're one of those people who have trouble sleeping, you may have seen one of those late night ads for the Scooter Store. These commercials are really compelling, because they essentially say, "Hey seniors, if we can't get Medicare or your insurance to cover the cost of your scooter .... We'll give it to you for free!"

Isn't that amazing? They have got to be really confident that Medicare is going to pay for these scooters or they could never make that kind of an offer on television. They'd go broke if they did! But because they know that Medicare does such a great job paying for active seniors with mobility problems, they can afford to make that claim to thousands of people.

And with that kind of commitment by Medicare, it's easy for seniors to get comfortable thinking that Medicare will be there to pay all of their long-term care bills. So where do all the problems start? Right when you step over into the next stage of health. Because if your mobility issues worsen to the point where need some in-home assistance, which can cost $15-$20 per hour, Medicare no longer covers you.

Maybe you live alone, or your spouse is frail and can't lift you, and you need to hire someone to come to your home and help you get out of bed, or help you bathe or get dressed, or check your insulin levels, or stay with you for an hour so your spouse can have a little break. Medicare doesn't cover these situations. They aren't paying anymore and you have to pay for that yourself. I wonder what JFK would think of that?

And what happens when you go further along and your health declines and it's not safe for you to stay in your own home anymore? Maybe you need to move to an assisted living facility where there are no stairs, and you can get more care in a safe environment with people to monitor and check on you; make sure you don't wander away; make sure you eat and take your medicines on time. Well, Medicare doesn't cover that either. The cost at this stage can be $2,000 to $5,000 per month, depending on how much assistance you need. Who can afford to pay that bill every month without going broke in a hurry?

What becomes of the fragile senior whose health care needs require 24-hour skilled care? This may be your spouse with advanced Alzheimer's or dementia, who must be monitored at all times for her own safety; or your husband who is bedridden and can no longer communicate. Does Medicare cover your nursing home bill, which on average costs about $6,000 every month? You guessed it – not at all. At those prices, it is very easy to see how a family's entire life savings can be wiped out in a matter of months.

Although another government program called Medicaid may assist you with your nursing home bills, you won't get any help until you have spent most of your own money first. That's right – the government will force you to spend so much of your own money, that by the time help arrives you may be left with almost nothing, despite the fact that you've paid taxes and social security all these years. Unless you have a plan, the government has a plan for you – spend down your life savings and then we will help you!"

Dick was losing his temper. "I don't know how much more of this I can take!"

Jane gently placed her hand on Dick's shoulder. "I know it's hard, but we need to hear it."

"You need to hear it, and I love talking about it!" Sarah Self-Pay said – way too happily for Dick's taste. But he let her continue.

"So where can you turn for help when Medicare doesn't cover you? Many turn to Medicaid, which is a government program designed to pay the health care expenses of the impoverished. That's right, when your government health insurance plan (Medicare) doesn't cover you; the next available option is Medicaid, a government program that won't help you at all until you spend down your nest egg.

In fact, check out this painfully true quote from Robert L. Kane, Professor of Long-Term Care and Aging at the University of Minnesota School of Public Heath: "We have facetiously described the American approach to paying for long-term care as universal coverage with a deductible equal to all your assets and a co-payment equal to all your income."[12] That is not a pretty picture, is it?

Medicaid is misunderstood on many counts. Because of the similarity in names, it is often confused with Medicare. Medicaid is a government program that provides financial assistance to seniors to pay for nursing home costs and a limited amount of home health care. The greatest share of nursing home residents – currently about 2/3s – pay their skilled nursing home bill with money from Medicaid.[13]

While Medicaid is a federal program, it is administered by each state, often with conflicting, confusing and inconsistent results. This is probably why the National Academy of Elder Law Attorneys has referred to Medicaid as one of the most complex laws of the United States.[14] Rules vary from state to state.

Remember Steve and Joan? If Joan turns to Medicaid for help with Steve's nursing home bill, chances are she won't get any help until she has blown through at least half or more of their own money first.

So what happens when you need Medicaid to help pay your nursing home bill? To qualify for Medicaid nursing home benefits, an applicant must meet three eligibility tests.[15]

1) Category test: Applicants must be at least one of the following: age 65 or older, disabled, or blind.
2) Income test: In most states, the applicant is required to "spend down" the majority of their monthly income as a co-pay to the nursing home.
3) Asset test: The Medicaid applicant is allowed to own only minimal assets. In most states this is capped at $2,000 for an individual. The spouse of the applicant is limited in their assets as well. As of right now, in Metropolis the spouse can protect up to $66,480 of countable assets. (Rules are the same in Columbia. Please remember: different states can have different rules.)

Regardless of the income and asset limits, Medicaid will not help you in any state until you prove that you are financially needy. Certain assets are exempt, meaning Medicaid won't consider them resources available for payment and won't count them toward your allowable asset limit. Most assets, however, are not exempt and will be counted against you.

Below is a brief (and somewhat simplified list of assets that are exempt in most states:

- Personal belongings (jewelry and furniture for example)
- One automobile
- Burial plots
- Some pre-paid funerals
- $1,500 of life insurance. This one can be tricky.
  Suppose you have a life insurance policy with a $100,000 death benefit and a surrender value of $23,000. You've been paying the premium for years because you want to pass this money on to your spouse or children when you die.
  But if you apply for Medicaid, the $23,000 will be considered a resource to pay the nursing home. Before Medicaid will help pay your bill, you could be forced to cash that policy out and lose the death benefit, turning a $100,000 future benefit into $23,000 cash that must be spent down.
  This can be especially devastating to your spouse if her biggest means of support after your death is supposed to be that big life insurance policy that you've been paying for years and years.
  - Your principle residence is typically exempt while you are alive up to a maximum of $500,000. If the applicant's spouse resides in the home, it is considered an exempt asset. But this is a tricky exemption. If the spouse at home decides to sell the house, they could turn an exempt asset into a non-exempt

countable asset, and the sales proceeds may be considered available resources that are subject to a Medicaid spend down."

Sarah Self-Pay paused here before continuing, "Here's one of my favorite parts. The truth is that **your house is never really safe when you are on Medicaid.** If the deed to your house is in you or your spouses name and one of you is receiving Medicaid, it is at risk."

Dick was depressed. "Okay, I admit that listening to the other retirement villains was bad, but none of them were as painful as this!"

Sarah Self-Pay jumped up with excitement. "Oh, thank you! You just made my day! And here's one more piece of depressing news I can't wait to share with you: pretty much any other asset is considered available for the Medicaid spend down – and you will be expected to use it. All your CDs, money market accounts, retirement accounts, stocks, bonds, most annuities and any other 'nest egg' type of accounts will be considered countable resources that can disqualify you from Medicaid benefits unless they are spent down.

As of February 8, 2006, our government came after the senior population once again! This law severely restricted the ability of senior citizens to transfer their assets, changing the "look-back" period from 3 years to 5 years.[16] This act even imposes harsh penalties for innocent gifts to family or donations to churches and charities. *This law changed the starting date of all transfer penalties, moving it up to the date of application. The result: no gifts are safe until five years pass from the date of the gift.*

Gifts that you make when you are healthy and not even remotely considering the possibility of future nursing home care can come back to haunt you if you become disabled within the next five years."

At this point Sarah Self-Pay stopped. Her smile seemed to get bigger and bigger as the conversation passed. Now it was as if her smile was as big as her face.

"Well we need to do something about this," Jane blurted out.

Dick nodded. "That's a good point. If we've learned one thing in the past day, it's that there are tons of problems out there, but there are solutions too. So what can we do to protect ourselves?"

Sarah Self-Pay laughed yet again. "Why in the world would I have any interest in telling you about that?" She asked with a devilish grin.

"Look honey," Jane said to Dick, "There's sunlight coming through the blinds. It's morning already. Why don't you give Tommy a call and invite him over for breakfast?!"

Dick smiled. "That's a terrific idea. I'll call him after I do one other thing."

"What's that?" Jane wondered.

"First I have to tell our villain friend here to get lost!" Dick said with his own devilish smile on his face. He sensed that the retirement villains were unable to stay when they were told to leave. At just that instant, Sarah Self-Pay gasped and was taken away in a cloud of smoke.

Jane gave her husband a big hug. "You're certainly getting the hang of this."

Dick smiled. "I better call Tommy!"

"Wow that was delicious!" Tommy exclaimed after putting down 3 eggs, 2 pieces of bacon and 3 buttermilk pancakes. "Brenda's been visiting her family for almost a week now, and you know that means I've been eating cereal for breakfast each day since!" Dick and Jane understood and smiled.

"Okay let's get back to work," Tommy said, "You were visited by Sarah Self-Pay. She covered all the horrible news about the costs of health care in retirement, right?" Dick and Jane nodded yes. "Okay good. At least I get to tell you that there are some things you can do.

There are a few strategies that can help you save money and avoid becoming impoverished, even if you are facing an immediate nursing home crisis and have been told you must spend down. But the government is never going to inform you of those money-saving techniques. Medicaid caseworkers are not even permitted to give financial or estate planning advice that could be beneficial to you. It's up to YOU to get informed and take action to preserve your life savings.

Changes in Medicaid laws make asset protection planning more difficult every year. The clock is ticking, and NOW is the best time to devise and implement your game plan. Remember, any transferring of assets or similar strategies should not be done without first seeking proper financial planning and legal advice. This is no area for amateur night!

So what are your planning options? Here are a few of the most commonly used options:

• Use your own assets. You can use your cash, stocks, IRA's, home, etc., to pay for a nursing home stay.

• Transfer assets out of your estate more than 5 years before anyone applies for Medicaid, and then let Medicaid pay.

• Buy Long Term Care Insurance.

- Invest in Asset Based Long Term Care Insurance.
- Do Asset Reposition Planning.

Let's look at each of these individually.

Buying long term care insurance may prove to be the best option for you. You buy enough insurance to cover the risk of going into a nursing home, just like you buy auto insurance to cover the risk of getting into an accident. Even if you eventually decide to take a pass, and risk paying for a nursing home yourself, possibly wiping out your entire net worth, you should at least investigate the different kinds of policies available to you before making a decision. Many retirees automatically assume that they can't afford long-term care insurance. But, unless you've taken the small effort required to see what's available...how can you know?

For those that do decide to buy it, they need to be careful with long term care insurance salespeople. They sometimes push for you to add on lots of features to your policy to raise your premium which then raises their commission!

Obviously, you don't want your 'advisor' working against you! This is just another example of why you want someone you can trust as opposed to working with an insurance or financial salesperson. Instead, the best approach is usually to simply to cover the most amount of the risk for the smallest possible premium.

That usually means few or no bells and whistles. Do you know what else that means? Instead of going broke paying for insurance, the bill could be around $100 per person per month. Now that of course depends on your age and health, but it gives you an idea of what's possible.

For some retirees, asset based long term care insurance is the most appealing option. Here's how it works: you have to make an initial investment. By doing so, you ensure that you will never have to pay any monthly or annual premiums. Then, if you need nursing care at any time in the future, the policy pays for the care for you just like a traditional long term care policy would. However, if you never need nursing care, your family is guaranteed to receive money back from the insurance company when you pass away. So, no matter what happens, you're guaranteed to get some kind of return on your money. Here's a quick example:

Take Doris: When she was 65, she invested $50,000 into asset based long term care. If she ever needs any nursing care, she will have over $312,000 of care that can be paid for by her policy. In addition, if she never needs nursing care, when she dies, her family will receive over $104,000 from the insurance company. While this isn't a perfect fit for everyone, many people find it to be a great option.

Now, if you choose not to get any kind of insurance, current Medicaid guidelines do allow you to protect more of your assets. The challenge is that this requires some specific planning on your part. This is what SuperRetirementPlanner calls Asset Reposition Planning. Basically, if you need to enter a nursing home, proper planning can help protect some of your life savings. BUT THIS REQUIRES SPECIALIZED PLANNING!

If you choose not to buy insurance protection, you should strongly consider getting professional assistance. ONCE AGAIN, DON'T TRY TO DO THIS ALONE. This is a very viable option, but this type of planning MUST be done exactly right. Getting advice from experienced professionals is the best way to avoid falling victim to one of the biggest risks to retirees: health care costs and the government programs designed that pay-or don't pay -for them."

"Is that it?" Dick asked.

Tommy chuckled a little. "Yep, that's it."

"Hmmm…" Dick was pondering what he had just heard. "It sounds like there's not a simple solution to this problem."

"That's a great observation Dick," Tommy said, "It definitely depends on each person's situation; and that's why working with a professional is so important."

"Point taken and I couldn't agree more!" Dick said. "Alright, we're up, we've had a great breakfast. Why not keep going?"

"Point taken and I couldn't agree more!" Tommy said with a wink and a smile. "It's a beautiful day outside. Why don't we head out by your pool?"

This question made Jane smile. "Tommy, do you think we should go out by the pool because the weather is so nice? Or is there some other reason?"

Tommy was definitely enjoying himself. "Don't you wish you knew?" Jane would have to wait just a little longer to learn the answer to her question.

END NOTES

1. LONG TERM CARE: Our Next National Crisis? A Think Tank Sponsored by the National Endowment for Financial Education, Scottsdale, Arizona – May 6-8, 2000.
2. PBS healthcare crisis: long term care. www.pbs.org/healthcarecrisis/longterm.html
3. Bureau of Economic Analysis, printed in Investors Business Daily, 1/25/05
4. How Will Baby Boomers' Retirement Affect Stocks?, USA TODAY, 7/19/2010
5. Elder Boom Will Be Felt Worldwide, US News & World Report, 7/20/2009

6. Containing US health care costs: what bullet to bite? – Cost Containment Issues, Methods and Experiences. Health Care Financing Review, Annual 1991 by Stephen F. Jencks, George J. Schreiber.
7. Containing US health care costs: what bullet to bite? – Cost Containment Issues, Methods and Experiences. Health Care Financing Review, Annual 1991 by Stephen F. Jencks, George J. Schreiber
8. Sue Stevens, "The Ins and Outs of Long-Term Care Insurance," Morningstar.com, September 29, 2005.
9. Spending Is Out Of Control, Business Week, 11/14/2005
10. Medicare Coverage of Skilled Nursing Facility Care, Centers for Medicare and Medicaid Services, 9/2007
11. Lyndon B. Johnson is credited with ultimately passing the Medicare bill into law in 1965. In fact, Medicare was the brainchild of John F. Kennedy, and was the focal point of his campaign. President Kennedy began the fight for Medicare in 1961, yet after an 18 month battle was unable to drum up the necessary support in the Senate, where his Medicare bill was defeated 52-48, due to vehement opposition by the AMA. *Health Care Reform: Revising the Medicare Story, POLICY AND MEDICINE, 12/1/2008*
12. *The Retirement Myth,* Craig S. Karpel
13. Nursing Homes: Cost and Coverage, AARP.org; 2007.
14. Medicaid: The Issue, www.naela.org/broc_Medicaid.aspx, NAELA 2008.
15. http://www.cms.gov/MedicaidEligibility/downloads/1998-2011SSIFBR061511.pdf
16. P.L. 109-171 Sec. 6011, 6014 (DRA 2005).

Chapter 6

Wall Street Greed

"Fortunes are made on Wall Street by catering to your greed. Not a penny is to be made protecting you from Wall Street's greed. That's your job."

Wall Street Versus America: The Rampant Greed and Dishonesty That Imperil Your Investments, by Gary Weiss

Tommy, Dick and Jane made their way straight to the pool in the backyard. It wasn't an elaborate setup, but gave Dick and Jane all they wanted behind their home: a place to relax, entertain friends, and beat the heat of the notoriously hot Metropolis summer days.

On the way to the pool, Dick and Jane were whispering back and forth. This made Tommy smile even more.

"Okay Tommy," Dick said as they all slid into their patio furniture right next to the pool, "Jane and I are dying to know. The next retirement villain must have something to do with the pool. Do they like to swim or something? I hope it's not a piranha!"

Tommy laughed. "Sit down and relax. It's not a piranha. It sounds like you're ready to keep moving. You were right that the pool is involved. But it's not that he *likes* the water. It's because he *needs* the water."

At that moment, a cloud of smoke appeared at the edge of the pool at the water's surface. This time in addition to the cloud of smoke, Dick and Jane noticed a very cool breeze along with it. When the smoke faded away, Dick and Jane could see nasty looking man icey

white and blue tights and a cape…almost like a superhero. His hair looked like solid ice, and he held a large gray gun.

"I'm not sure who this villain is," said Dick, "But if you always bring that cool breeze with you, you can stop by any time!"

Tommy frowned at Dick's comment. "I hope you enjoy the laughs while you can, Dick, because this retirement villain could decimate your portfolio if you allow him to."

"Thanks Tommy!" The ice man bellowed, "It's nice when people give credit where credit is due for a change!"

Dick was confused. "What are you, made of ice? What in the world does that have to do with our retirement?"

"Good observation." Tommy calmly answered, "Forgive me for not making a proper introduction. Dick and Jane, this is Iceberg Ivan. So, yes, he is made of ice. But he doesn't represent the cold, or freezing, or ice. As you can tell from his name, he got his name because of icebergs."

Dick was still confused. "Okay, so he could sink our retirement like it were the Titanic?"

"Let me clear this up Tommy!" Iceberg Ivan quickly said, "You see Dick, I think it's safe to say you know what a regular chunk of ice is. But an iceberg is a unique type of chunk of ice. The reason the difference is important is that an iceberg is far more than what meets the eye. In fact, according to www.Wikipedia.com, a typical iceberg only has $1/9^{th}$ of its volume above the surface. So the point I'm trying to get to is I'm a *whole* lot more dangerous to you than you realize!"

Jane was quickly getting the point. "Okay that makes sense. But how exactly do you hurt our retirement? It's obviously not by cooling down the water in our pool!"

"Well said Jane," Tommy replied. "Iceberg Ivan represents fees on your nest egg. You probably know what I mean here. They can take on all sorts of names and appearances: account fees, maintenance fees, management fees, wrap account fees, advisory fees, early withdrawal penalties, and the list goes on and on."

Dick and Jane nodded in agreement. At one point or another since they started saving for their retirement, they had paid many of the types of fees that Tommy listed. "Okay," Jane said, "I've got my notepad and pen ready. I think we're ready to hear all about Ivan and these fees."

Iceberg Ivan looked over at Tommy who nodded back at him. "Very well," said Ivan, "I'm pretty sure you're not going to enjoy this as much as I will!"

While Ivan lived off of hiding most of his fees, he couldn't help but savor the chance to explain just how badly all those fees can hurt retirees. "I'm sure you understand that companies that hold your savings and investments are going to charge you fees since that's obviously the business that they're in; and some fees can be extremely reasonable. But we've got waaaaay too much to cover to give those any time. What we're going to talk about are the types of fees that can wipe out half of your nest egg slowly and silently. They are far more significant and dangerous than originally meet the eye."

"Like icebergs!" Jane interjected.

Ivan always enjoyed when his listeners were getting the symbolism he represented. "Very good! These types of fees are almost always being charged on investment accounts. Stocks and bonds – things like that. Many people are familiar with mutual funds, so I'll use them in most of my examples.

Now, I have done some pretty amazing work decimating peoples nest eggs with mutual funds. But before we discuss those fees in great detail, let me show you an example of how devastating these can be. Tommy even helped me develop a couple of slides to make it easy to follow.

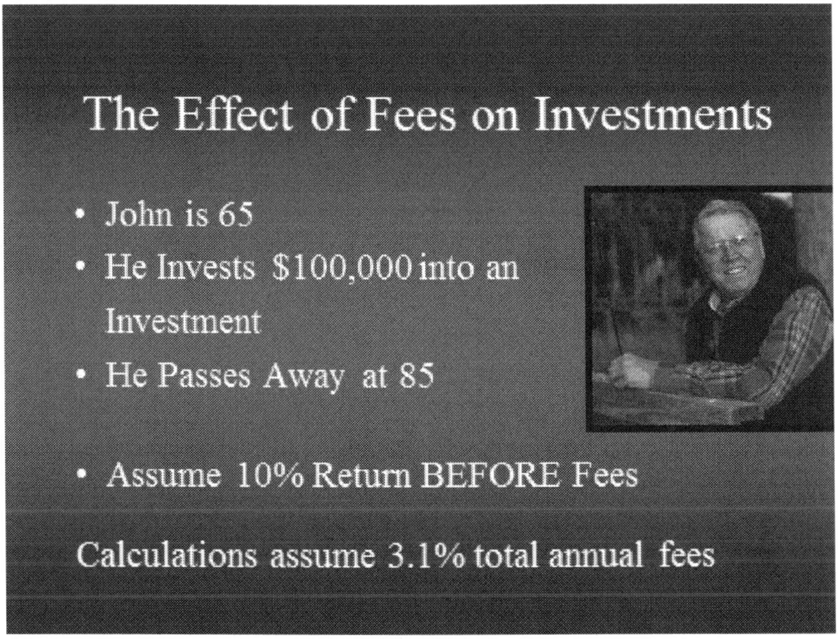

The Effect of Fees on Investments

- John is 65
- He Invests $100,000 into an Investment
- He Passes Away at 85
- Assume 10% Return BEFORE Fees

Calculations assume 3.1% total annual fees

Figure 6-1

In this example, John is 65 and he has $100,000 in what many would consider to be an average cost investment portfolio. I'll explain more about what that means later. To keep my math simple, I'm assuming he passes away 20 years later at age 85 and he's reinvesting all his gains each year.

"Now, we're going to assume he is getting 10% return but that's before the fees. So he's actually earning a little less than 7% a year after fees. Over 20 years, we would certainly expect that money to grow substantially. In fact, in a hypothetical 0% fee account, John's original $100,000 would grow to $672,000."

"Wow!" Jane exclaimed, "That's a lot of money!"

Iceberg Ivan nodded. "Yes it is, but wait until you see what happens after the fees! You see, those fees cost John a little over $3,000 in the first year. But just 3% a year lowered his value after 20 years all the way down to about $358,000. Check out this handout." (See Figure 6.2)

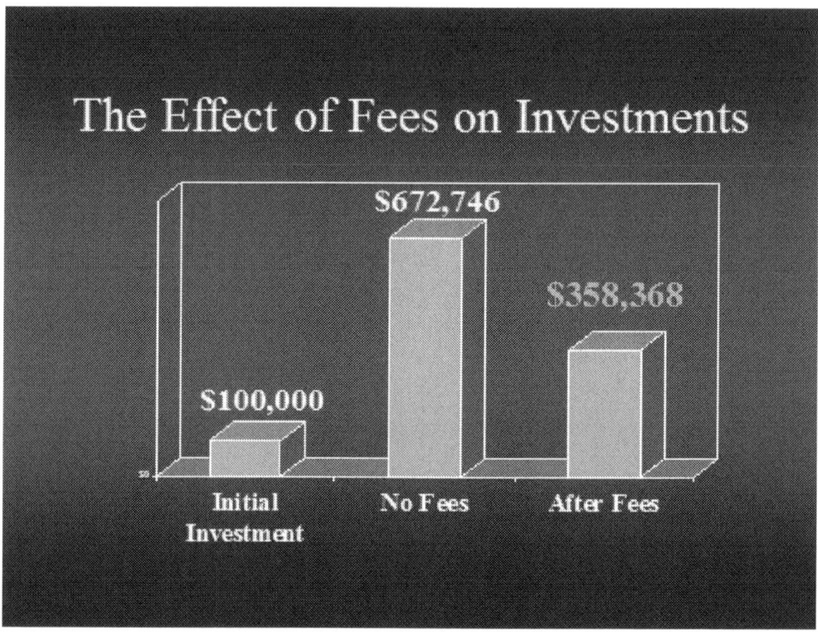

Figure 6.2

Dick was in total disbelief. "$358,368?! You better check your math buddy! You said he's being charged about 3% per year on his investments, right?"

"Yes, that's exactly right," replied Iceberg Ivan with a knowing nod. He'd seen thousands of retirees make this math mistake before. "Okay," Dick continued with his thought, "If he's being charged around 3% a year on his investments, how can his balance be reduced at the end by almost half. There's no way in the world *about* 3% can turn into *about 50%!*"

Iceberg Ivan displayed a gentle smile. Sarcastic, but gentle. "Believe me Dick, I feel your pain. But unfortunately for investors, it's true. You see, there is tremendous power in the effects of compound interest. However, the cost of fees on your account *also* compounds over time. The longer you have your money invested, the greater the difference is between what you could have had and what you're left with."

Jane's concern became much worse. "Uh oh; and Lady Longevity already covered the fact that we might be retired for 30 or more years."

"Oh yeah!" Iceberg Ivan exclaimed, "That kind of time gives me the chance to *really* do some damage to your nest egg! Let me ask you, are you familiar with the founder of Vanguard, John Bogle?"

Dick nodded in the affirmative.

Iceberg Ivan continued, "Mr. Bogle has fought for years to educate investors on the dangers of investment fees. Here's a fabulous quote of his relating to how this works:"

> *"You the investor put up all the money and you take all the risk but collect only 53% of the profit. The system puts up no money, takes no risk but collects 47% of the return. Almost half the profit siphoned away by those who had everything to gain and nothing to lose."*[1]

"That's unbelievable," stammered Jane.

"That's disgusting!" announced Dick.

"I know!" said Iceberg Ivan beaming from ear to ear. "I hope that makes it clear why the fact that I'm an iceberg makes so much sense!"

Tommy had let Ivan go on for some time, and he felt like it had gone on long enough. "Okay Ivan. Why don't you tell them a little bit about how Wall Street is able to get away with all this."

Ivan's smile quickly faded. After glaring at Tommy for just longer than necessary, he turned to Dick and Jane and said, "Something told me you would make me do that. Alright, here's how it's done:

The easiest way for me to explain this is with quotes from some of the most respected people who have studied investment fees. For example, as Gregory Baer and Gary Gensler wrote in their book, *"The Great Mutual Fund Trap:"*

> *"There's a reason you don't consider the costs of investing, of course. Mutual funds and brokers have constructed a system where the costs are practically invisible."*

As much as I hate to admit this, Baer and Gensler are absolutely correct. Most investments have found ways to make fees practically invisible. I say practically invisible because those fees typically have to be disclosed in a prospectus. Of course, almost every retiree has told me that a prospectus is about as readable to them as the U.S. tax code!

What it boils down to is that the fees are taken out of your account over the course of the year, and you never see it on your statement."

"He's right," Jane interrupted, "I've tried to look at our statements before, and they never say what we're paying. I knew there was no way they were working for free."

"Oh that's a good one!" Iceberg Ivan exclaimed with a hearty laugh, "No they certainly aren't working for free. I won't bore you with all the details, but let me quickly explain where that 3.1% per year average fee number I used earlier came from. It's been referred to in many books, articles, radio and television shows, but Richard Rutner summarizes it best in his book, *"The Trouble with Mutual Funds:"*

> *"Expense ratios average 1.6% per year, sales charges 0.5%, turnover generated portfolio transactions costs 0.7%, and opportunity costs-when*

> *funds hold cash rather than remain fully invested in stocks-0.3%. The average mutual fund investor loses 3.1% of his investment returns to these costs each year"*

Dick was quickly losing his temper. "Wait a minute! Are you telling me that my investment company has been making over 3% a year off of me and they don't even have to show it on my statement? My retirement account is about $500,000. 3% of $500,000 is $15,000 a year. That should be illegal!"

"Hold on there Dick," Iceberg Ivan responded, "Your company may not be charging you that much. That's just the average. Your company may be charging you much less!"

"OR they may be charging you much more!" Tommy said. He wasn't going to let Ivan leave out part of the truth!

"I feel sick," Dick said, "And you already made the point that $15,000 a year is chump change compared to what it will cost me if I leave the money in there over a number of years. These fees could end up costing me hundreds of thousands of dollars!"

Tommy nodded. "Believe me Dick, I was just as shocked as you. In fact, when I did the math, I figured over my retirement, investment fees could easily cost me over a million dollars! Ivan, read to Dick and Jane some of the quotes from experts urging people to move away from these types of high fee investments."

"Awww, you're no fun!" Iceberg Ivan replied. "Okay, here are a few of the ones Tommy always wants me to include. I guess we could start with best-selling author Ric Edelman. This is from his book, *"The Lies About Money:"*

> *"Just as I gave you the truth about money in my first book, I must now alert you to the lies that are placing your financial security in jeopardy. You need to become aware of these lies so that you can avoid the pitfalls they create.*

And there's no greater pitfall than the one created by the mutual fund industry. There's no other way to say it: The industry is ripping you off. You are incurring greater risks, lower returns, and higher fees than you realize, and as a result, you are in danger of not achieving your financial goals.

The situation is shocking – and no one is more astonished than me. My firm, one of the largest and best-known investment advisory firms in the nation, has placed $4 billion of our clients' assets into mutual funds. I've been the mutual fund industry's biggest proponent.

No longer. Jean and I have now sold all our investments in mutual funds. All my colleagues at Edelman Financial have done likewise, and our clients are following our advice. You need to sell all your mutual funds too.

Excuse me for being blunt, but the fact is that the mutual fund industry is now flush with liars, crooks, and charlatans. Daily business activities include deceit, hidden costs, undisclosed risks, deceptive trade practices, conflicts of interest, and fundamental violations of trust – all at your expense. Since September 2003, the mutual fund industry has paid out more than $5 billion in fines, and more than eighty executives have been barred from the industry or thrown in jail. Despite this, state and federal regulators say that investors are still being abused.

There are many variable costs for operating mutual fund, and these are excluded from the expense ratio. Indeed, a study by Wake Forest University, the University of Florida, and the Zero Alpha Group found that 44% of mutual fund fees are not disclosed in the prospectus.

The biggest of these omitted costs is trading expenses. Whenever the mutual fund manager buys or sells a security, he pays brokerage commissions (just like you would if you bought or sold a stock or bond).

But to find them, you must look in the fund's Statement of Additional Information, an arcane document that's even bigger, denser, and harder to read than the prospectus – and which fund companies, stockbrokers, and brokerage firms are not required to give you.

I'm sure you share my outrage over the mutual fund industry's behavior. But is that enough of a reason to sell your mutual fund?

Most people would say yes. But some might take a different view. As long as the mutual funds keep producing profits, they're willing to tolerate the scandals.

Well, the profits aren't there. Mutual funds are simply no longer able to consistently generate above-average returns. … By being unable to offer consistently good performance, mutual funds can't justify their expenses – especially after they've been caught with their hands in the cookie jar.

No wonder that the highly regarded David Swensen, chief investment officer of Yale University's $15 billion endowment fund, wrote in Unconventional Success: A Fundamental Approach to Personal Investment that there is "overwhelming evidence that proves the failure of the mutual fund industry."

Mr. Swensen is right. The industry's ethical breaches are not only insulting to us as investors, but they have caused you and me real economic losses. …I no longer tolerate the situation. We've sold all our holdings of mutual funds. You should too."

"Speaking of David Swensen," Iceberg Ivan continued, "He has been considered by many to be one of the most successful portfolio managers of the last 20 years. Here are a few more of his comments from his book *"Unconventional Success:"*

"The failure of the mutual fund industry to produce attractive investment results stems from the inherent conflict between behaving as a fiduciary and acting as a profit-maximizer. The contest between serving investor interests and making money never even makes the starting gate. Profits win in a runaway.

> *Fees contribute substantially to the gap between investor aspirations and performance reality. The mutual fund industry levies an assorted collection of charges, including up-front loads, contingent deferred sales loads, standard management fees, distribution and marketing assessments and incentive payments. The aggregate of the compensation paid to mutual fund managers virtually guarantees that investors fail to achieve market-beating results.*
>
> *In the final analysis, the benefits of active management accrue only to the mutual fund management companies, not to the investor. Asset managers profit, while investors lose."*

"Here's another great quote," Ivan pushed on, "from author Gary Weiss in his book *"Wall Street Versus America: The Rampant Greed and Dishonesty That Imperil Your Investments:"*

> *"Mutual funds dare to be average. In fact, they dare to be lousy. If you had shares in a mutual fund on January 1, 1984 just as the bull market was taking off, and held on to it until December 31, 2003, the chances are better than 90 percent that your fund failed even to match the performance of the Standard & Poor's 500 stock index. Now, if that's not a repudiation of perfectionism and all the agita that comes with it, I don't know what is.*
>
> *Contrary to the prevailing wisdom of personal-finance journalism, buying into a mutual fund is not a "prudent" and "sound" exercise in "portfolio diversification." It is actually a "dumb" and "asinine" exercise in "paying people to do a lousy job of managing your money." You pay them handsomely to be mediocre, and you even pay for the ads in which they proclaim, and you pay for the flacks and data vendors who sucker the media to co-proclaim, that they do not stink but actually do an outstanding job in managing $8 trillion and counting of your money.*
>
> *Mutual fund companies cheerfully overcharge you for inflated fees and expenses, trade too much, pay through the nose in commissions, and overpay their pals in the brokerage industry in return for office space, research, and other perks, with you footing the bill. They are not neurotic or hesitant as*

they overcharge you. They confidently charge you fees that they don't deserve whether they are making or losing money, and they have job security that would make a postman envious.

The real mutual fund Scandals are straightforward. The real scandals involve Sunday school morality and simple concepts, such as "taking." The money is there, so they take."

Dick sighed. "This is all making me sick to my stomach. It feels pretty hopeless. I sure am hoping that you're going to tell us that SuperRetirementPlanner can help us with this."

"Oh good grief!" Iceberg Ivan shouted, "The last thing I want to do is hear about *that* guy!"

Tommy couldn't help but smile. "Goodbye Ivan! Now we're going to talk about how to fight you!"

As soon as Tommy finished talking, a cloud of smoke appeared at the edge of the pool, and when it had faded away, Ivan was gone.

Jane was ready for answers and had her pen and paper ready for notes. "Okay Tommy. Tell us what we can do to fight the iceberg!"

"Jane," Tommy responded, "I love your excitement; but the truth is that SuperRetirementPlanner can answer that question much better than I can. I can tell you that he was able to show me all kinds of investment options that didn't require me to pay all those annual management fees.

He'd be the first to tell us that the accounts that I'm in may or may not be the best kind for you. So as much as I know you'd love answers right now, I think its best just to say that the good news is that there are some great options out there. It'll be up to you to review them with SuperRetirementPlanner and determine which are best for you."

"That makes total sense," Dick replied in a calm tone, "Okay, so let's see, we've met Lady Longevity, the Invisible Enemy, Evil Uncle Sam, Sarah Self-Pay, and now Iceberg Ivan. You said there were seven retirement villains, so I guess we've still got two more we need to deal with. I don't know about you two, but I'd love two things right now: to hurry up and meet these two, and to get out of this hot sun!"

END NOTES

1. *Battle for the Soul of Capitalism,* John Bogle

Chapter 7

Is *This* the Biggest Lie of the Brokerage Industry?

"Retirewent: what happened to the retirement hopes and dreams of Americans after the meltdown."

- Gregory Salsbury, Ph.D., *Retirementology*

Dick, Jane and Tommy hopped out of their patio chairs and went inside. Dick wasn't alone. Not only were they all eager to keep moving through the retirement villains, but since Iceberg Ivan had left, the hot summer sun had become virtually unbearable.

Dick and Tommy headed straight for the living room and picked out a couple of comfortable chairs – Dick naturally in his favorite recliner. Tommy faced him on a loveseat. Jane joined them a few minutes later with some lemonade and glasses she had grabbed from the kitchen.

"Oh, Jane, thank you so much!" Tommy said when Jane arrived.

Jane was happy to do something nice for Tommy. "Tommy, ti's the least I can do. You've helped us so much in such a short amount of time. I'm starting to feel like we finally understand this stuff."

Tommy smiled. "I'm so glad to hear that Jane; but remember, we still have two more retirement villains to meet. Don't get cocky on me!" Tommy had been enjoying sharing such valuable information with his friends and couldn't help teasing Jane just a little.

Jane recognized the smirk on Tommy's face. "Don't you worry Tommy. We're ready for the next two." She finished pouring the three drinks, handing one to both Tommy and Dick, and took a sip for herself. "Alright," she said while putting her drink down and picking up her pen and pad of paper, "Who's next?"

Tommy leaned toward them. "Very well. I feel I should warn you. I know I've said that each of the villains is important. But this particular villain is extremely sneaky and could wipe out an entire nest egg. Oh, and don't be alarmed when he gets here."

Dick and Jane looked at each other. "Don't be alarmed," Dick said, "sounds like this retirement villain is going to be something else!"

At that exact moment, a cloud of smoke appeared in the middle of the living room. Dick, Jane and Tommy kept their eyes focused on the smoke. As it faded, they could all see the next retirement villain. Even though Tommy had warned them, Dick and Jane were indeed alarmed; because standing in front of them was a wolf!

"Guys," Tommy quickly started, "I told you do NOT be alarmed. He can ruin your nest egg, but he doesn't physically bite you! Allow me to introduce your next retirement villain, Systematic Sammy."

Systematic Sammy was indeed an intimidating presence. He stood on his hind legs, was very muscular, and most importantly, had an evil grin on his face.

"Pleasure to meet you!" Systematic Sammy started, "Let me tell you a little about myself. As Tommy said, my name is Systematic Sammy. Yes, I am a wolf; and Tommy is right. I don't physically hurt you. Instead of crushing you in my jaws, I love to crush your nest egg!"

Dick and Jane were letting this sink in. As shocking as some of the retirement villains had been, none had been this physically frightening. Dick could sense that while Jane understood intellectually that Sammy wasn't going to attack them, she was still frightened.

Dick was eager to get this encounter over with. "Alright, let's move this along. What does Sammy represent and how can he hurt us?"

Tommy nodded. "Good idea. Let's get right to it. First, what does he represent? Systematic Sammy represents a particular type of financial advice. Imagine your advisor invests your money in the stock and bond market. After you retire, your advisor recommends you keep your investments the same and take money out of your nest egg each month to live off of. That type of withdrawal is called systematic. With me so far?"

Dick and Jane nodded.

"Great," Tommy continued, "The reason this villain is a wolf is because wolves are notorious for being something different than they appear. Of course you've heard stories of wolves dressing themselves up in sheep's clothing to trick the sheep."

"Hey!" Systematic Sammy interjected, "I resent that analogy – I don't attack sheep!"

"I know, I know," Tommy said, "Bear with me." Tommy turned his attention back to Dick and Jane. "A sheep appears harmless right? That's the same as taking a withdrawal once a month out of your nest egg. It actually seems logical, right? However, it's really a wolf in sheep's clothing. Taking a systematic withdrawal could actually wipe out your entire nest egg!"

"Wow," Jane was finally able to gather herself and join the conversation, "That sounds horrible. I hope you have an example so we can better understand this."

Tommy looked at Systematic Sammy. "Okay," Systematic Sammy said, "I can take it from here. There are actually a couple of ways I can show you. Let me start with a fairly straightforward example.

Assume you had $100,000, and you invested it for 10 years. We'll assume you earned an average of 6% a year. Also, each year you withdrew 6% a year. Okay, so you start with $100,000. Earn an average of 6% per year. Withdraw 6% per year. What would you have left at the end of the 10 years?"

Dick and Jane looked at each other. "$100,000," they responded simultaneously yet hesitantly.

Systematic Sammy flashed a knowing smile. "Exactly. That's what everyone says, and that's why I'm compared to a wolf in sheep's clothing – because it's a trick question.

The trick to the question is that I didn't tell you that you would earn 6% every individual year. I said you would earn an '*average* 'of 6% per year. If you DID earn 6% each and every year, your answer would be correct; but if your return goes up and down each year but ends up averaging 6%, you may very well have an *extremely* different value at the end of 10 years than $100,000.

Look at this handout I brought with me. (Figure 4.1) If you had a couple bad investment years to start, have solid investment years through year eight, then have terrific investment years in the last two years, you would still earn an *average* of 6% per year. At the end of 10 years, your $100,000 has fallen all the way down to $35,612. Yes, that's right; you earned an *average* of 6% per year, withdrew 6% per year, and managed to lose way more than half your money in only ten years!"

Is Average Return the Biggest Lie of the Brokerage Industry?

Year	Beginning Value	Withdrawal	Return	Ending Value
1	$100,000	-$6,000	-30%	$65,800
2	$65,800	-$6,000	-20%	$47,840
3 to 8		-$6,000	10%	
9	$33,828	-$6,000	20%	$33,394
10	$33,394	-$6,000	30%	**$35,612**

Figure 4.1

Dick was in complete shock. "That's unbelievable! It's just like you said Tommy – it sounds so logical, but the person in this example is going to go broke! Why does that happen?"

Tommy opened his mouth to answer, but Systematic Sammy put his paw in front of it. "Tommy, I know you're going to tell them anyway, and I'd rather it came from me. It boils down to this:

If you have your nest egg invested in anything that changes value – such as something tied to the stock and bond markets – that investment is probably changing in value at least once per day; but when you are retired you need income every month; and for most people, that income is going to be the same every month. So let's say your investments go down in value the first month you're retired. Are you willing to skip getting your income that month?"

"That's ridiculous," Dick quickly said, "you just said that I'd be retired. We'd have to have that income to live on."

"Exactly," Systematic Sammy said, "So you're going to take your income; but your investments have lost value. That means you're forced into selling them when they are down. I'm sure you've heard the expression that you make money in the stock market by buying low and selling high, right?

Well, in this situation, you've bought high and sold low. The exact opposite of what you're supposed to do. As you can see from the simplified example we just covered, every single month your account drops, it forces you to sell lower than what it was worth the previous month.

Now, I've done such an amazing job of convincing people that this is a great idea that I bet even most financial advisors have bought in on my little plan. If most financial advisors fall into doing this for their clients, just imagine how many millions of retirees I can try to bankrupt!

In fact, I can actually give you a real life example from print!"

The Most Dangerous Retirement Advice?

"Back in 2001," Systematic Sammy continued, "the *Miami Herald* had a certified financial planner that regularly contributed to the paper. In the December 2nd, 2001 edition, they printed this question and answer to and from the planner:

> *"Question: I am 70 years old and retired, hoping that my IRA would sustain me when the time came. Since I have to begin withdrawing next year, I would appreciate your advice. I was advised several years ago to invest my IRA in mutual funds. For a while it was great, but along with so many other people, I have lost a great deal in the last two years. Should I take my losses and reinvest in a secure savings even though the interest rates are low?*
>
> *Answer: If ever there was a time to stick with the plan, it's now. The ups and downs of the market are to be expected, and if you've been an investor for more than a few years, you've ridden a few waves yourself; mostly up markets, just no down markets this long and nasty. I feel your pain, but 2 percent CD's and no growth aren't going to cut it.*
>
> *Check your funds and make sure they're solid and leaning more to the conservative growth and growth income funds. Aggressive funds tend to be more volatile. Instruct your custodian to send you your required minimum distribution monthly by selling shares of your funds. This is called a systematic withdrawal and it works like a charm."*

"Oh my goodness!" Exclaimed Jane, "that's exactly what you told us was the wrong way to take money out!"

Systematic Sammy broke into a huge, devilish smile. "I know! It's absolute music to my ears! And as a retirement villain, it makes me so happy that investors believe that systematic withdrawals always work AND so do many financial salespeople."

Tommy wanted to jump into the convsersation. "He's right. It's scary to me because that type of advice can be so dangerous. Before Sammy continues I want to point something out. Let's look at one part of the article again:"

> *"Instruct your custodian to send you your required minimum distribution monthly by selling shares of your funds. This is called a systematic withdrawal and it works like a charm."*

This type of advice made Tommy really angry. "This is flat out, completely and totally WRONG! Well, it's not 100% wrong," Tommy admitted, "Technically, if the value of the funds NEVER went down, the advice would be correct. If you can find me a mutual fund that never goes down, please let me know!

The phrase should have read: "This is called a systematic withdrawal and it works like a charm as long as you have chosen the right mutual fund and the stock market always goes up faster than you are drawing the money out."

Dick laughed. "That's a good one! I wouldn't need a financial advisor if the stock market always went up!"

"Thank you!" Tommy was thrilled that Dick was just as irritated as he was. At this point he realized he should settle down and let Systematic Sammy continue. "I'm sorry Sammy. You can continue now."

Systematic Sammy, like all the other retirement villains, was in no hurry to explain all the in's and out's of systematic withdrawals for

Dick and Jane. "Sure. I guess a good place to go to would be a quote. This is from the book *Probable Outcomes,* by Ed Easterling:

> *"Some advisors or planners will go so far as to advocate that today's long-term retirees invest heavily in the stock market. Those pundits say, "A market that has never lost money over thirty-year periods won't let you down in the future." It's true that there has never been a thirty-year period when stock market investors overall have lost money, yet there have been quite a few thirty-year periods that have bankrupted senior citizens who were relying upon their stock portfolios for retirement income."*

"And I'm happy to report," Systematic Sammy proudly summed up, "the reason the stock market has bankrupted senior citizens is the volatility of the market during times of withdrawals for income."

Tommy was watching Dick and Jane. To him they seemed to be following along quite well. He felt the problem with systematic withdrawals had been explained in good detail. While Systematic Sammy was still there, he wanted to make sure they covered one more topic.

How Risky IS the Market?

"Okay," Tommy started, "Let's cover one more thing. The reason a systematic withdrawal can harm you so badly is because stock and bond markets ARE volatile. So Sammy, please explain exactly HOW volatile the markets can be.

"You got it boss!" Systematic Sammy said, "You need to understand two things: HOW volatile the markets can be, and HOW MUCH that can affect you. Another quote from *Probable Outcomes* explains this well:

> *"During the period 1900-2009, the simple average of the annual gains for the stock market, excluding dividends, was 7.1%. The compounded*

annual gain excluding dividends reflects a more accurate view of realized annual returns at 4.7% over the 110 years.

The difference between the average return and the compounded return is the result of two effects denoted by Crest Mont Research as "volatility gremlins." These volatility gremlins can reduce the dollars you actually receive by more than 90%! By understanding their impact, investors can appreciate the benefits of reducing volatility and increasing the consistency of investment returns. Investors can then realize higher compounded returns, and experience a more enjoyable and less stressful investment ride."

"Let me stop there," Systematic Sammy said, "So over 110 years, the stock market *average* annual return was 7.1%, while the *realized* annual return was 4.7%."

Dick was both a little confused as well as upset. "That's what I thought you said! So whenever we see advertisements showing a great average return, that doesn't actually mean we'll earn that much money?"

Tommy nodded. "That's correct. Unless your account earns exactly that return EACH year. The bottom line is how the author summarizes this section. Investors that can reduce volatility and increase the consistency of returns can realize higher compounded returns and enjoy a less stressful investment ride."

Jane chuckled. :Isn't that what everyone wants anyway?!"

Tommy laughed. "You're certainly not the only one. That's what Brenda and I want, and I imagine most retirees want too! Keep going Sammy."

"Very well," Systematic Sammy continued, "Here's a little more detail on how damaging volatility can be from *Probably Outcomes:*

"The first volatility gremlin is the impact of negative numbers on compounded returns. To illustrate the effect, consider an investment over two years. If an investment portfolio makes 20% the first year and loses 20% the second year, the simple average rate of return is zero. The investor, however, has actually lost 4%. To break even, it takes a greater positive return than the offsetting negative loss. For a -20% loss, the offsetting gain is +25%. It works the same whether the positive or the negative occurs first. A +25% gain can be wiped out by a -20% loss.

The second volatility gremlin is the impact of the range of returns on the average. As the returns in a series become more dispersed from the average, the compounded return declines. Keep in mind that half of all years in the stock market occur outside a 32% range, from -16% to +16%. As the level of dispersion increases, the impact from the second volatility gremlin increases".

Tommy didn't want Systematic Sammy to skip over this important point. "So basically what the author is saying is, your goal should be to reduce volatility, and if you can, eliminate it; and I'm sure you can imagine, Mr. Easterling isn't the only person making that recommendation. In fact, the man who many would consider as the most successful investor of the past 40 plus years, Warren Buffet, has said:

"Rule No.1 is never lose money.

Rule No.2 is never forget rule number one."[1]

"I hate that one," Systematic Sammy said, "Here's another quote – this one is from author Edward Winslow in his book *Blind Faith: Our Misplaced Trust in the Stock Market, and Smarter, Safer Ways to Invest:*

"The primary objective of an intelligent investment strategy should be to preserve capital and build upon it at a consistent, moderate rate in both bull

and bear markets. Our personal definition of risk is simple and understandable: we don't want to lose money."

"Oh, and let me give you one more quote from the previously mentioned *Probable Outcomes:*

Too often, investors have been led to believe that hope and faith in the long term are appropriate investment strategies. Investments should seek to make money, not simply to passively participate in the markets. Toward that end, the first rule of making money is to avoid losing money. Risk management is not just about enhancing success; it is about avoiding the unacceptable failures.

"Finally," Systematic Sammy summarized, "here's another helpful quote. This one is from best-selling author Harry S. Dent in his book *The Great Depression Ahead:*

"The key insight is not to accept the proposition that investors cannot, or should not, take steps to guard against losses. As an investor, it is your money, your future, and your responsibility to protect yourself in the best way possible."

Dick looked over at Jane and grabbing her hand, "Okay, I think it's safe to say that all makes complete sense to us."

Tommy nodded and smiled. "I thought you might say something like that. There's one more topic I'd like Sammy to cover. While certainly no one can predict what the stock market will be like in the future, Sammy, please give us a quick rundown on what some economic experts are saying."

Tommy had just about pushed Systematic Sammy over the edge. "Tommy, I will cover that, but nothing more!"

Tommy nodded at Systematic Sammy and then smiled at Dick and Jane.

Systematic Sammy began on this final topic, "Alright, let's get this over with. The previously mentioned Harry S. Dent is a good place to start. In his book *The Great Depression Ahead,* which was just published in 2009, Dent sees a pretty grim number of years ahead of us. One of the quotes in his book is:

> *"There will be a substantial bear market rally, likely between around mid-2012 and early to mid-2017. The Dow should reach as low as 3,800."*

"3,800!" Dick literally jumped out of his favorite recliner. "That's hard to even imagine! That's way less than half of what it is right now!"

"I agree," Systematic Sammy said, making his best effort at being *Sympathetic Sammy*. "Of course, it's just one man's prediction. If you'd like details of why he sees that in the future, it's all in his book.

How about a quote from Jeffrey Hirsch. Jeffrey's father Yale Hirsch is widely credited as being the first to predict the massive stock market increases of the eighties, and Jeffrey worked with his father from 1986 until Yale's passing in 2001. This is from Jeffrey's 2011 book *Super Boom:*

> *"I concur with the general concept of restrained economic growth and a lid on stock prices over the next several years. I believe we will flirt with the lower end of the markets range during that time. A test of the lows in the Dow 6,500-7,500 range in the 2012-2014 time frame is entirely in the cards."*

Another author who has analyzed the markets and is pessimistic about the future is the previously mentioned Ed Easterling. Let's first review his outlook, then his recommendations for investors. These are also comments from his book *Probable Outcomes,* which was just published in January of 2011:"

> *"The reality is that the current secular bear market likely has a long way to go, both in terms of magnitude and time. It could last a decade or longer with mediocre returns, or end in a blaze of fury within five years or so."*

Tommy interrupted again, "Sammy, again, I don't want you to skip anything important. So the author believes the next five to ten years will be a bear market. How does he suggest investors plan for this?"

Systematic Sammy snarled and took a step towards Tommy. Fortunately, Tommy had seen this before and knew Sammy couldn't physically hurt him, so he stood his ground. Systematic Sammy glumly responded, "Here's another quote from the same book:"

> *Secular bear markets are not periods during which to avoid investing; they are periods that demand an adjustment to investment strategy. The implication for today's investor is that the likelihood of financial success in retirement is considerably less than most pundits advocate.*

Systematic Sammy savored the last sentence. "That's right, the likelihood of financial success in retirement is considerably less than most pundits advocate. Doesn't that just have a great ring to it?"

"Sammy!" Tommy yelled as he was losing patience.

"Alright!" Systematic Sammy said, "Here's what Mr. Easterling recommends for retirees in the same book:"

> *"Retirees who want to withdraw 5% or more will need a more consistent and higher return profile for their investments than passive investments in the stock market or bond market can provide. The principles of absolute return investing are important for preserving capital and generating much-needed returns."*

"Once again the author is advocating avoiding volatility. By recommending "absolute return investing," Mr. Easterling is saying avoiding losses should be paramount. Now, let's lastly look at the author's comments for those getting ready to retire:"

> *"Near-Retirees (within a decade or so of retiring) will be called Late Accumulators. The appropriate strategy for investors in this group needs to start with assumptions based upon reasonable expectations. The stock market is not positioned to start a secular bull ascent or achieve even historically average returns. This group of people has a sobering near future, one that requires wealth preservation rather than wealth accumulation. In a decade or two, this group will likely realize solid returns from the next secular bull market – the goal is to have all, or more, of their current savings available to invest. Great returns generated from half as much capital can still deliver a disappointing lifestyle in retirement."*

"I don't care what you all think about it, but come on, "this group of people has a sobering near future" – isn't that the best?!" Systematic Sammy was not going to miss one last chance to take a jab at them.

"Enough already!" Tommy exclaimed, "Sammy, get out of here!" Before Systematic Sammy could even respond, a cloud of smoke enveloped him and he disappeared.

Dick was relieved to have Sammy gone. "Thank you! Okay look, we get it. Systematic withdrawals from accounts that can lose value and taking too much risk with our nest egg can be dangerous. Plus, some experts believe the coming years could include some significant risk in the stock market. So is the solution to just take all our money and put it into CD's? Or a savings account? Or better yet, how about under our mattress!"

Tommy knew Dick was frustrated, but he also detected a twinkle in his eye while he was talking. "Dick, I'm glad you can laugh a little at this. To answer your question, no, you don't need to put all your money under your mattress; and I know you're eager to hear some better solutions. I have to ask you for just a little bit of patience. You see, we'll get into some possible solutions when we meet our final retirement villain."

"Okay," Dick said, "I can live with that. But why do I have to be patient? Why don't you just call up the last villain right now?"

Tommy smiled. "Well, he doesn't make house calls, so we have to go to him; but if you're interested, we can go see him right now. It's only about a 10 minute drive."

Dick and Jane responded in unison, "What are we waiting for?"

END NOTES

1. wikiquote.org/wiki/Warren_Buffett

Chapter 8

Is There a Better Way to Invest?

Creative thinking may simply mean the realization that there is no particular virtue in doing things the way they have always been done.

– Rudolph Flesh

Within minutes, all three of them were in Dick and Jane's Buick and on the road.

"So where are we heading?" Dick asked as he started his car.

Tommy couldn't help smiling because he knew exactly what the follow up question would be. "The museum of American history."

"Why in the world would we go there?" Jane asked before Dick could.

"I knew you'd ask that!" Tommy replied, "it's a pretty simple answer – that's where are last retirement villain is; and rather than ruin the surprise, why don't we just leave it at that until you meet him?"

Dick started to object but decided it wouldn't do any good. Besides, it wasn't far away. Throughout the drive, he racked his brain trying to remember the exhibits in the museum - which he hadn't seen for years.

They quickly arrived at the museum. Dick paid for their admission, and they made their way into the exhibits. "Alright, I give up. Who is it?"

Tommy chuckled at Dick's urgency. "Thank you for your patience! He's actually right behind you."

Dick and Jane quickly turned around. They saw an exhibit from the days of cave men. There were a number of men around a fire pit. Not real men of course, but mannequins.

"I don't get it," Dick said, "Come on out retirement villain!"

The obligatory cloud of smoke immediately appeared enveloping the exhibit. When the smoke settled, a man dressed in nothing but a loincloth greeted Dick and Jane with a series of loud grunts.

Even after meeting all the other retirement villains, Jane was startled. "Wait a second. Aren't you the mannequin?"

"Andy," Tommy calmly answered, "I'll take this. Dick and Jane, allow me to introduce you to your final retirement villain. This is Antiquated Andy. Please understand that Andy is a cave man, and therefore he can't talk for himself. Oh, and don't worry about his club. He isn't here to hit you with it, he's here to represent the damage he can do to your nestegg."

"Okay," Dick started, "I'm definitely sensing some symbolism here. Andy is Antiquated. This is dealing with something old?"

Tommy let out a belly laugh. "Nicely done Dick. You're absolutely right. Andy represents big brokerage investment advice that for some brokers hasn't changed for many generations. The world goes through massive change, and their advice stays the same. Investors go through massive change in their lives, yet the advice from these brokers stays the same. I'm sure you can see that this type of advice

could be dangerous! So since Andy can't help us, let me go ahead and give you the whole story.

Have you ever owned a brokerage account? Have you ever met with or worked with a stockbroker? There's an incredibly high chance that regardless of who the broker was, or what company they worked for, I have a pretty good guess at what they recommended that you invest in.

Now don't get me wrong: I'm not saying that all brokerage firms are bad, and I'm not saying that all stockbrokers are bad. Not at all. I AM saying that some brokerage firms and brokers haven't changed their advice very much over the past 100 years.

In these antiquated allocations, almost all the money is invested in one way or another in one of three places:

1. U.S. Stocks
2. U.S. Bonds

3. Cash

Now I say one way or another, because there are all kinds of ways to invest in those three areas: individual securities, mutual funds, ETF's, and all other sorts of options. But they're all usually made up of those three things. And guess what? Those are the same 3 things some brokers were selling decades and decades ago!

The good news about this Wall Street approach is that it works…sometimes. It works assuming the following three conditions:

1. The economy and stock market are generally doing well. You know, like much of the '80's and '90's.
2. You have enough time to ride out any downturns, and
3. You aren't drawing income off the account. I'll assume you haven't forgotten about Systematic Sammy already, right?!

It should be clear to you that this approach could be hazardous to your retirement!

Fortunately, there is an approach that is time tested that could be a much more retirement-friendly way for you to invest. The method I'm referring to is often called the Endowment Model of investing. It's named for the numerous college endowments that have popularized this style. Since implementing this style back in the '80's, these endowments have shown a remarkable ability to generate above average returns while typically enjoying much less volatility than the stock market. Let me tell you more.

The September 26th, 2007 issue of SmartMoney magazine featured an article by James B. Stewart on this subject titled "A League of Their Own." In his article, Mr. Stewart covered numerous important areas in a short space. Let's take a look at some of the most helpful portions here:

> *In recent years investors have eyed burgeoning Ivy League endowments like high school seniors applying to Harvard and Yale with weak grade point averages, low SAT scores and no extracurricular activities: zero chance of getting in. Can you blame them for being envious? In the year that ended June 2006, Yale notched a 22.9% return. Even more impressive is its consistency. Over the past 10 years, which included the market meltdown of 2000 to 2002, Yale has had annualized gains of 17.2%. Harvard, meanwhile, boasts a 10-year average of over 15%.*

Andy, you remember the market meltdown of 2000 through 2002. Was your strategy able to bankrupt some retirees nest eggs?"

Andy got REALLY excited. A huge smile came to his face, he tossed his club down on the ground and started pounding his chest, jumping up and down and gruntly loudly. Dick and Jane both took a couple of steps back out of shock.

Tommy had to quickly stop him. "Andy enough! I'm really sorry about that guys. Sometimes I forget that he can act like a cave man. Okay, back to the facts. Check out this first handout. Through the Harvard endowment's fiscal year 2010, it had easily returned better than a portfolio made up of 60% stock market and 40% bond market holdings. Of course, this comparison assumes the investor earned the returns of the stock and bond market indexes, and Iceberg Ivan obviously showed you how unlikely that would be!

Historical Investment Return
Annualized for Periods Greater than One Year

	Harvard Endowment Model	60/40 Stock/Bond Portfolio*	Harvard's Comparison**
5 years	4.7%	2.1%	>123%
10 years	7.0%	2.0%	250%
20 years	11.9%	7.8%	>52%

* S&P500 / CITI US BIG
** A mathematical comparison

This updated report incorporates information from Harvard University's Financial Report for Fiscal Year 2010 Dated 10/15/2010.

Figure 8.1

So the endowment returns during that period were excellent. There are still two smart questions to ask: 1) Can their strategies be duplicated? And 2) Are they risky? Let's go back to Mr. Stewart's article:

> *Of course, Harvard and Yale have long enjoyed formidable advantages. Even other institutions have been hard-pressed to keep up, let alone individual investors. Surprisingly, that may be beginning to change. We've taken a close look at these endowments and at the new investment vehicles now available to the rest of us. Our conclusion: Even average investors can mimic Harvard or Yale in their portfolio, with access to some of the Ivy League's most exclusive and esoteric asset classes.*

These comments may not seem like that big of a deal to you, but they are game changers. You see, SOME of the assets the endowments invest in were difficult to impossible for the typical investor to take advantage of for decades. This has changed. Back to Mr. Stewart:

> *As (former Harvard endowment manager Jack) Meyer puts it, "The most powerful tool an investor has working for him or her is diversification. True diversification allows you to build portfolios with higher returns for the same risk."*

Ah! Now we come to that second question I mentioned: How risky is it? So Jack Meyer claims better returns without additional risk. Doesn't this sound too good to be true? I don't blame you. After all, that's how investing is supposed to work: Low risk, low return. Higher risk, potential for higher returns. Let's see what else we have in Mr. Stewart's article:

> *(Yale Chief Investment Officer David) Swensen agrees that diversification should be the "bedrock" of every investor's portfolio. "Most investors, institutional and individual, are far less diversified than they should be," he says. "They're way overcommitted to U.S. stocks and marketable securities." If you haven't been following the Ivies' investment strategies over the years, you may be surprised by how Harvard and Yale allocate their endowment assets. Their portfolios are most likely radically different from yours, or from the models advocated by most financial planners, which are still heavily weighted toward traditional asset classes like stocks, bonds, and cash. What's most striking about their portfolios today is how little they have invested in U.S. stocks and bonds.*

This section sheds some light on the situation. The claim is better opportunity for higher returns without more risk. So the endowments are clearly doing something different. And what are they doing? Some might call it radical. I'd say so. After all, many on Wall Street have been telling us for generations that the path to success is what? Diversifying in stocks, bonds, and cash. Yale and Harvard have come along and defied Wall Street; and some claim they have proven Wall Street wrong!

The idea of enjoying true diversification is worth diving into more detail. Swensen writes extensively about this subject in his book "Unconventional Success":

> *In spite of nearly universal support among investment professionals for well-diversified portfolios, market practice generally fails to reflect fundamental portfolio management precepts. Consider the average asset allocation of college and university endowments, which represent the best managed of institutional funds. Ten years ago (1993) domestic equities constituted nearly 50 percent of assets (48.6%) and domestic bonds more than 40 percent (40.8%). With two asset classes accounting for almost 90 percent of assets, the portfolios flunk the test of diversification. In the early 1990s, college and university endowment managers earned dismal grades.*
>
> *Contrast the experience of the broad group of colleges and universities with the best-endowed educational institutions. Harvard, Yale, Princeton, and Stanford lead the endowment world in size and led the endowment world with early adoption of well-diversified portfolios.*

In his book, Swensen goes on to show the breakdown of investments held by these four esteemed endowments. On June 30, 1993, on average they held over 44% of "diversifying assets." On June 30, 2003, on average the percent of diversifying assets had increased to over 68%. This is quite a difference from holding almost 90% in U.S. stocks and bonds! In his book, Swensen summarizes this way:

> *The well-diversified portfolios produced superior results. Real-world application of fundamental investment principles produces superior outcomes.*

Now, going back to James B. Stewart's article:

> *As might be expected at big research universities, this aggressive move away from traditional assets was rooted in academic research suggesting that investors can earn a higher long-term rate of return with less risk by diversifying beyond the traditional mix of stocks and bonds. Economists James Tobin and Harry Markowitz each won a Nobel Prize for work they did on this topic while at Yale.*

So this is clearly not theory. Yale and many other endowments have been using these strategies going back as far as 1985.[1] The returns since then as well as reduction of ups and downs are proof. Academically and with real portfolios, the endowments have had proven success. Let's go back to the comments about Harry Markowitz. He published his work on diversification in 1959 which has had an enormous effect on investing ever since.

Unfortunately, Wall Street often uses Markowitz's research to recommend U.S. stock, bond, and cash portfolios and nothing else. Maybe these recommendations were made years ago because there were no cost effective ways to use additional diversification back then. Or maybe Wall Street had different reasons…or motives.

Regardless, what could possibly be the reason Wall Street continues the same recommendations they've made for the past 50+ years? Laziness? Ignorance? Greed? All of the above? Author Raymond J. Lucia, CFP has an opinion in his book, *Buckets of Money:*

> *"Why does Wall Street gravitate toward the asset-allocation method? The answer is actually quite simple. It's simple, profitable for the firm, and easy to implement. It's easy to charge a wrap fee on 100 percent of a client's assets.""*

Dick and Jane had been very quiet. Through spending so much time with the retirement villains, they had learned a whole lot more when they kept their mouths shut. At this point, however, they sensed that Tommy had reached a natural break in his explanation.

Dick decided to ask what he thought was an obvious question, "So if they aren't investing in U.S. stocks and bonds, just exactly WHAT are they investing in?"

Tommy smiled because was happy that Dick had asked such a good question. "This handout shows a recent snapshot of the Harvard Endowment Fund's holdings. Of course, their investments are always changing, but this gives you a general idea.

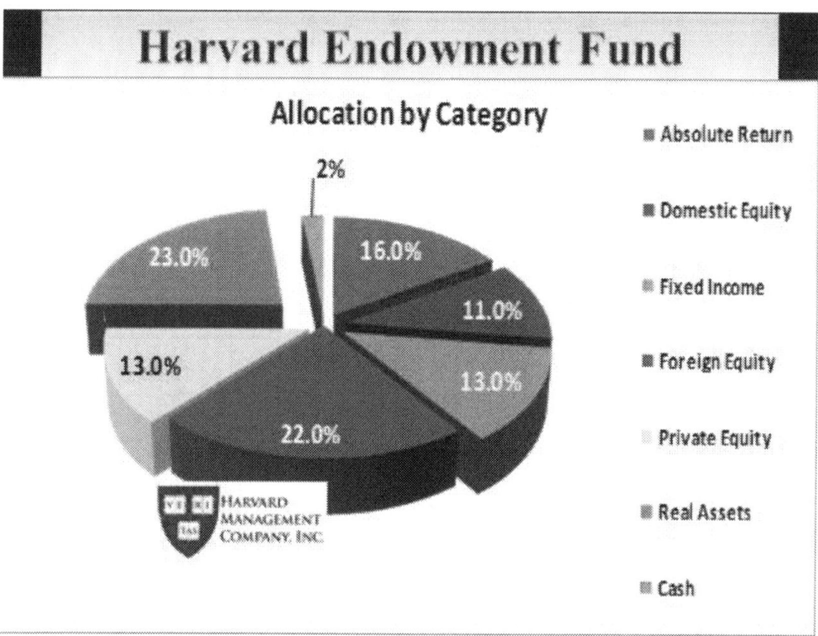

Figure 8.2[2]

In this particular example, the endowment fund is only holding 26% of its assets in those three traditional areas:

1. U.S. Stocks: 11%
2. Bonds: 13%
3. Cash: 2%

Before we get into some of their other holdings, we should spend a moment on WHY the endowment doesn't invest more in these areas. Bonds in particular are an area where Harvard's David Swensen speaks passionately. The following is also from his book "Unconventional Success":

> *"Sensible investors avoid corporate debt, because credit risk and callability undermine the ability of fixed-income holdings to provide portfolio protection in times of financial or economic disruption."*

That's a pretty strong statement, isn't it? Let's briefly review his reasoning from the same book:

> *"Unfortunately for investors, corporate bonds contain a variety of unattractive characteristics, including credit risk, illiquidity, and callability.*
>
> *Callability poses a particularly vexing problem for corporate bond investors. The holder of corporate bonds faces a 'heads you win, tails I lose' situation. If rates decline, the investor loses the new high-coupon bond through a call at a fixed price. If rates rise, the investor holds a now low-coupon bond that shows mark-to-market losses.*
>
> *The best outcome for holding bonds to maturity consists of receiving regular payments of interest and return of principal. The worst outcome represents default without recovery. The asymmetry of limited upside and unlimited downside produces a distribution of outcomes that contains a disadvantageous bias for investors."*

Tommy had to laugh. "Okay, I'll admit it: Mr. Swensen tends to dress up his language just a little more than I do! Here's how I'd sum up that last paragraph: Mr. Swensen believes corporate bonds in general provide way too many risks and offer way too few benefits; and below is how Mr. Swensen sums up his thoughts on bonds:

> *"Investment-grade corporate bonds, high-yield bonds, foreign bonds, and asset-backed securities contain unattractive characteristics that argue against inclusion in well-constructed portfolios."*

That's pretty straightforward; and his comments make so much sense. Why should you bother to use them in your portfolio if they don't benefit you?

So what types of investments DO the endowments typically invest in? Let's look at the categories listed in the Harvard Endowment handout we looked at a moment ago:

- Foreign Equity, which is 22% in Figure 8.2. This makes sense, right? While there are certainly unknowns overseas, it's difficult to argue there isn't opportunity.
- Private Equity, which is 13% in Figure 8.2. This category can be tougher for the individual investor to get into, but could be a good fit for some. In short, private equity is investing in much smaller, private companies. As it may sound, this can offer much greater potential returns as well as significant risk!
- Absolute Return, which is16% in Figure 8.2. Absolute return generally means it keeps a priority on maintaining positive returns regardless of how the economy or stock market are doing. Sounds pretty logical doesn't it? Many would argue this category is FAR more important to a retiree than it is to someone investing for retirement in their 20's or 30's.
- Real Assets, which is 23% in Figure 8.2. This is one of the easiest categories for the individual investor to duplicate. Real estate, for example, can be invested in through multiple different methods and in relatively amounts. Is it an important area to use in your portfolio? Once again let's see what Mr. Swensen has to say in his book "Unconventional Success":

  "Investments in real estate expose investors to the benefits and risks of owning commercial office properties, apartment complexes, industrial warehouse facilities, and retail establishments. High-quality real estate holdings produce significant levels of current cash flow generated by long-term, in-place lease arrangements with tenants. Sustained levels of high

cash flow lead to stability in valuation, as a substantial portion of asset value stems from relatively predictable cash flows. Returns covering the quarter century from 1978 to 2003 for an index of marketable real estate securities stand at 12.0 percent per annum."

Now you obviously haven't forgotten about the Invisible Enemy already, right?" Tommy asked Dick and Jane.

Dick gave Tommy a knowing look. "Come on Tommy, you know he made quite an impression on us. We won't forget everything he taught us about how dangerous inflation can be."

Tommy was glad to hear Dick's response. "Good! Well, that's another reason some experts like including real estate in an investment plan. Here's one more quote from Mr. Swensen's *Unconventional Success:*

"With its inflation-sensitive nature, real estate provides powerful diversification to investor portfolios."

Well, I think that about sums up the big areas I wanted to cover. I know Andy loves to be able to get out of the exhibit and stretch his legs, but I think it's time to send him back."

Dick and Jane smiled at Antiquated Andy and Dick said, "Goodbye, Andy, it was nice meeting you, and even better learning how to avoid your tricks!" Antiquated Andy got a confused look on his face and instants later was swept up in a cloud of smoke before he could do anything. After the smoke had cleared, Dick and Jane saw that Andy had returned back to his place by the fire.

Jane was sad to see Andy go. "Tommy, Andy seemed so nice. Why did you get rid of him so fast?"

"I'm sorry Jane," Tommy explained, "I love Andy, and it hurts to send him a way. That's why I try to do it as quickly as possible. Plus, we've been through a lot together, and I still want to cover one last thought that should be important to you: is the endowment model a good fit for retirees?

Well, certainly the goal of achieving higher returns with less risk is appealing to everyone! So what's the catch? Generally, the endowment model does not provide as much accessibility of your portfolio as the old Wall Street model. So is that a problem for a retiree?

Well when you're retired, you certainly need to be able to use SOME of your money! But I hope you're not planning to use ALL of your nest egg all at one time, would you?"

Dick laughed. "If we use all our nest egg at one time, we'd have a pretty sorry looking future, wouldn't we?"

Tommy nodded. "Exactly; and as we talked about with Systematic Sammy, most retirees are looking to create income with their savings and investments. Well, you'll never guess who else is doing that…the endowments! That's right, those universities are taking income from the endowments EVERY year.

In fact, in 2010 Ivy League schools, on average, relied on endowments to fund more than 25% of day-to-day operations, with Harvard, Princeton, and Yale topping the range at 55%, 48%, and 37%, respectively.[3]

So in 2010, the Harvard endowment was providing 55% of Harvard's day-to-day income. I don't know what that sounds like to you, but to me that sounds an awful lot like a retiree using their nest egg to provide income to add to their Social Security and pension!"

"That really makes a lot of sense," Jane said as she was letting everything they had just learned sink in. "Okay, so we've met all seven retirement villains, heard why they can be so dangerous, and talked about strategies to use against them. It feels kind of strange that we don't have another one to expect to meet!"

"I totally agree honey," Dick said, "Tommy, does that mean we're done?"

Tommy smiled. "Not exactly. I know we've been through a lot, but on the way back to your house we have one last stop to make."

END NOTES

1. http://en.wikipedia.org/wiki/David_F._Swensen
2. Harvard Management Company Endowment 2010 Annual Report, 10/15/2010
3. Timothy J. Keating, The Yale Endowment Model of Investing is Not Dead, 4/20/10, www.RIABiz.com

Chapter 9

YOUR Retirement Income Plan

"You can get poor a lot faster than you can get rich."

- Bob Miller

Tommy was excited about the surprise he had up his sleeve for Dick and Jane. He directed Dick to an office complex just off the highway.

"An office park?" Dick wondered, "Tommy, you've got to tell us what we're doing here!"

Tommy chuckled. "Dick, you just can't appreciate a good surprise, can you?"

Jane shook her head no and laughed. "Nope. Never has, and I'm quite sure never will."

As Dick pulled into a parking spot, Tommy said, "Okay, let's get out quickly. I don't want us to be late for our appointment!"

"Appointment?" Dick and Jane asked inquisitively.

Tommy simply smiled as he led them into the office building. He took them straight to the office he knew well. He opened the door and smiled at the office manager who was there to greet them.

"Hi Heather," Tommy said, "How have you been?"

"Well hello stranger!" Heather replied, "It's great to see you!"

Tommy wasted no time making introductions. "Heather, I'd like to introduce you to my friends Dick and Jane. Guys, this is Heather. She basically runs the show around here!"

Heather smiled. "Don't you know it! Dick and Jane, it's so great to finally meet you! Tommy has told us a lot about you."

"Nice to meet you Heather," Dick replied, "I hope most of what he's said has been good!"

"What else *could* he tell us?" Heather quickly shot back, "Now, you all are here for your noon appointment right? You're right on time. Please follow me to our conference room."

Heather led them to a conference room and offered each of them a seat. "He'll be with you in just a minute," and she closed the door.

"He?" Dick questioned Tommy. Then he looked over at Jane and said, "Am I the only one who's confused?"

Tommy was loving it; but he knew he finally needed to let them in on who there were there to see. "Okay guys. I set an appointment for us with SuperRetirementPlanner. I hope you're excited!"

"SuperRetirementPlanner?" Jane wondered, "Yes, we're obviously excited; but I never imagined we'd meet him in a regular office!"

As she was talking, the door opened and a man walked in. "I know, I know," he said with a smile, "You were probably expecting a cape, tights, and for me to be flying through the sky, right? I'm SuperRetirementPlanner. Dick and Jane, I'm so pleased to meet you."

"It's great to meet YOU SuperRetirementPlanner!" Dick said as he and then Jane shook SuperRetirementPlanner's hand, "And yes, we were expecting something a little more, uh, more 'superhero-like'."

SuperRetirementPlanner smiled. "I totally understand, and it happens all the time. I think the name throws people off. When it comes to your retirement, your planner doesn't need to *look* like a superhero – but they *do* need to help protect you from those nasty retirement villains! I trust Tommy took you on a journey to meet all seven of them?"

Dick and Jane nodded yes.

"Great!" SuperRetirementPlanner said, "Well, Tommy filled me in a little bit on your background. Normally, my first meeting is designed more for me to get to know all about your current situation and what you want your retirement to look like; but because it seems like you've got a time sensitive situation, Tommy and I thought it would be best to spend a few minutes today jumping in on some details of creating a retirement income plan. Then, we can get together another time to discuss all the details of your situation…without Tommy of course!"

"That sounds wonderful," Jane said, "I'm glad I brought my pen and paper – fire away!"

"Perfect," SuperRetirementPlanner started, "Alright, hopefully you remember your time with Systematic Sammy where you learned about one of the most common ways to take income in retirement that can *devastate* your retirement; and I *do* mean devastate. I'm sure you agree that if a strategy is the primary reason you go from having a nest egg to being broke, that is flat out *devastating!*

Because of this, I believe that **Much of the Financial Services World Has Been and Continues To Do Retirement Income Planning WRONG!** Why do I say that? Think about the most common approach:

Step #1: Generate pages and pages of colorful pie charts and graphs representing various asset allocation models.

Step #2: At retirement, take a monthly withdrawal from the portfolio. We call this withdrawal 'pro rata.' That just means taking a portion from each type of investment.

Step #3: Every so often, rebalance the portfolio. This means that regardless of how the different areas of the portfolio are performing, by "rebalancing" them you are moving them back to where they started.

Many financial advisors, stockbrokers, online calculators, and mutual fund companies does it this way. But we've already talked about the problems with this method. The great news is that there IS a better way to generate retirement income with the goal of making sure you don't run out of money. Who invented it? I haven't got a clue! And I'm happy to admit up front that it wasn't me!

Before I go any further, let me give credit where credit is due. I learned just about everything I know about this strategy from three different financial planners: Michael D. Reese, Robert E. Grace, and Raymond J. Lucia.

Michael D. Reese is a super sharp financial planner in Traverse City, Michigan. Mike is primarily a financial advisor, but he also coaches other successful financial planners around the country. Back in 2005, I invested in Mike's coaching to learn about what he called "Income Scheduling," and it changed mine and my client's lives! We'll talk about that more in a second.

Next is Robert E. Grace. Bob runs a tax and financial practice out of Fort Meyers, Florida. I had the pleasure of meeting and learning from Bob in 2010. I invested in a two day program where Bob took us through his income planning process that he calls SIPS: the Structured Income Portfolio System.

Finally, there's Raymond J. Lucia. As I started working more and more closely with income planning, I found Ray's book: "Buckets of Money." This is an entire book about this strategy.

Regardless of the source, these guys are all talking about the same thing: a different way to take income in retirement; and it's not rocket science. You're basically separating your nest egg into short term money, medium term money, and long term money. Depending on your situation, you might separate it into three areas – or maybe four or five. Here at our office we call it your **Systematic Retirement Income Plan.**

But here's the most important point: **this has been proven to be a better way**. It's been proven academically, and it's been proven through all of our financial practices with real people! Let's quickly look at the academics first.

In June of 2007, State University of New York professors John Spitzer, Ph.D. and Sandeep Singh, CFA, Ph.D. had their article published in the Journal of Financial Planning. The article's title is "Is Rebalancing Your Portfolio During Retirement Necessary?" and it summarized their lengthy study into the different options for taking income in retirement.

The study showed that spending down safer accounts first before using more aggressive investments is the best way to take income. In fact, here is an exact quote:

> *"This method also is most apt to leave a larger remaining balance at the end of 30 years, while rebalancing leaves the smallest amount."*

Ray Lucia, who has used this strategy for his clients for 18 years, sums it up this way in "Buckets of Money:"

> *"Buckets of Money offers a reassuring – and scientifically proven – strategy that gives investors both growth and income. Thus, this strategy can shield you from the short-term ups and downs of the market. It'll give you the courage and discipline to stay invested no matter what the future holds. It'll help you plan your retirement years with greater confidence."*

Ahh, it's funny that Ray decided to use that phrase in his book: "*plan your retirement years with greater confidence.*" You see, that's our slogan around here: *"Retirement with Confidence."* Our goal is to always give you confidence in your retirement plan. As I mentioned, not only does the previously mentioned study show that this method is better, but Mr. Reese, Mr. Grace, Mr. Lucia and I all have many clients that have enjoyed the benefits for many years.

Now, some clients ask me why this approach isn't talked about more often or used more frequently. Let me read you one more quote from Ray Lucia's "*Buckets of Money:*"

> *"The strategy of spending down bonds or fixed investments first (Buckets 1 & 2) and stocks and real estate last (Bucket 3) was scientifically proven, based on solid academic research, to produce the best results. The so-called rebalancing method – the pie chart allocation with systematic withdrawals used most frequently by mutual fund companies, financial planners, and brokers – has now been proven to produce the worst results.*
>
> *So why does Wall Street and the financial-planning community gravitate toward the asset-allocation, rebalancing method? The answer is actually quite simple. It's simple, profitable for the firm, and easy to implement. It's easy to charge a wrap fee on 100% of the client's assets. With a Buckets of Money strategy, the fees charged may only be on 30% to 40% of the total assets, thus a firm would lose 60% to 70% in fees."*

You see, Mr. Lucia hits on some big points here. First of all, for a large international company, it makes things much easier on them if all their brokers use the same type of plan. However, I believe the biggest reason is Ray's last point regarding the fees.

Let's use an example. Let's say a couple retires and has $700,000 in all their savings and investments that they plan to use to create their retirement income. Many advisors and brokers will charge this couple what the industry calls a wrap fee to handle their accounts. This type of fee is based on the amount of money they oversee for you. A common wrap fee might be one to two percent per year.

That means that for this couple, the Wall Street company is receiving $7,000 to $14,000 *every year*. Ray's point is that using this strategy, those fees might be cut down to somewhere between $2,100 to $5,600 per year. I bet you can guess how many Wall Street companies are looking to take that big of a pay cut!"

Dick laughed loudly. "I'm pretty sure I know the answer to that one…a big fat zero!"

SuperRetirementPlanner laughed with Dick. "I agree! Now I'm not going to go into great detail today of how this type of plan works. For one, I know you've already had an exhausting couple of days; but most importantly, I haven't found out all the details of *your* situation and what *you're* looking to accomplish. So I don't think going into details at this time would be appropriate – but let me quickly give you the basics.

The first step will be figuring out everything that is unique to your situation:

- Your assets
- Your income needs, including when you will need to start to take income, how much income you'll need, if and when that income need will change, and how much we want it to increase to protect you from that nasty Invisible Enemy of inflation
- Your tolerance for risk and drops in your investment values, and most importantly,
- Your financial and retirement goals

Once I have all that, my job is figure out how your assets should be allocated and how you should take income from those assets. I think Ray Lucia's explanation is excellent. He keeps it simple by calling each type of investment area a "bucket." So let's imagine that your plan will include four buckets. Let's also assume that you are retiring today, so you need income right away. The first bucket will cover your income for the next five years so this needs to be a really safe investment. Typically this would be something that is guaranteed and insured.

Next, your second bucket will cover you for the next five years: six to ten years from now. This is where our clients' plans might start to vary more from each other's. Some of our clients have some low risk investments in this bucket. Others prefer to also keep this bucket filled with guaranteed investments.

Your third bucket is next. As you might have already imagined, it will provide you with income ten years from now – covering years 11 through 15. Since we're not touching your principle during the first ten years of your retirement, if you choose to, this is a place where we can start to add some risk to your portfolio.

Finally we have your last bucket. This bucket is designed for long-term growth. It can be filled with riskier investments. Or, you can choose to fill it with very long term accounts that offer a guaranteed growth rate. Since we don't expect to use your principle for such a long time, you might be surprised that even when interest rates are low, we can lock in some pretty good returns in this type of situation. This handout gives you an idea of a very simple plan.

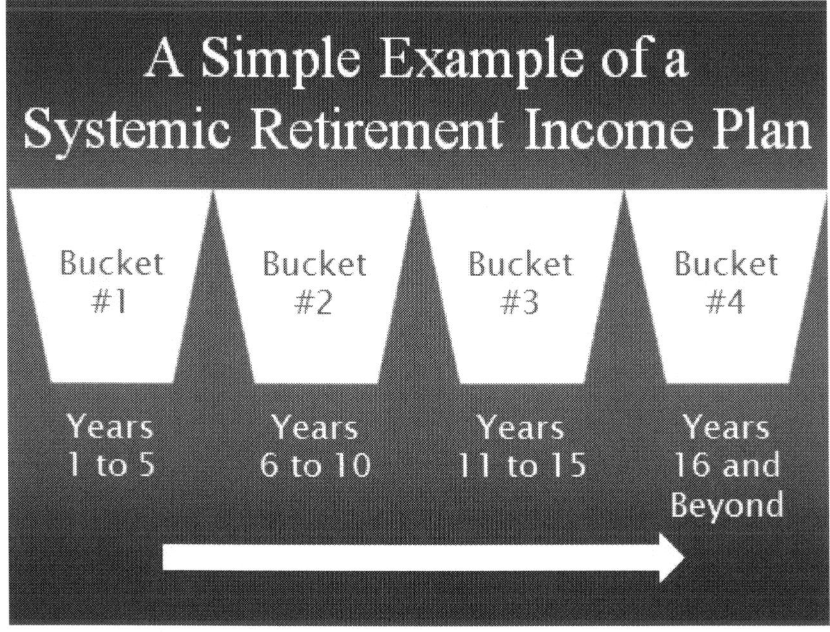

Figure 9.1

Please keep in mind this is a very simple example. It doesn't mean that you would only have one investment in each bucket. Depending on your plan, it could be one investment per bucket, or you could have a mixture of numerous investment vehicles.

Also, the fourth bucket is NOT designed to pay you income for a set number of years. Bucket four is designed to replace the money you spent during the first 15 years of your retirement; and typically, our goal is to replace ALL the money you spent over that time. So after fifteen years of enjoying your retirement and your steady income, you often still have as much money as you started with – or possibly more!"

"Wow!" Jane interrupted, "After meeting Lady Longevity and the Invisible Enemy of inflation, I was definitely worried about running out of money. Just having a chance to have as much or even more money left years later gives me a lot of hope!"

SuperRetirementPlanner always enjoying hearing his clients had hope. "Thank you Jane. It's certainly not a guarantee; but it's our goal. So that's a really quick overview of what we call your *Systematic Retirement Income Plan.* Basically, the goal is to set up your income so you always know where it's coming from, how much you're going to get, and where your income will be coming from in the future. We want it to end up being as much like your current paycheck as possible!"

Dick felt the urge to jump in, "I would think that would be what just about anybody would want as they get ready to retire." Everyone in the room nodded and Dick continued, "Tommy, thank you SO much for everything you've done for Jane and I. We will never forget it. SuperRetirementPlanner, thank you SO much for spending your valuable time with us. I am absolutely sure that Jane agrees with me when I say, what do we need to do to get moving on our own retirement plan? I think we are both very excited to be retiring with confidence!"

Tommy blushed from Dick's warm words. "You're very kind, and you're welcome. Helping friends of mine retire with confidence has been possibly the most rewarding experience of my own retirement! And SuperRetirementPlanner, I'd also like to thank you for your time."

"You're all very welcome," SuperRetirementPlanner said, "It's also incredibly rewarding for us! Dick, as far as your question goes, on your way out, please schedule a meeting with Heather. She will let you know all the documents we'll need you to bring so that we can begin putting together the best plan possible for you.

Oh, and I have one more piece of homework for you. Let me give you this report I've put together - I'd like you to read it before our next meeting. I call it *"Ten Steps to Helping You Save YOUR Retirement."* It gives you some simple ideas I'd like you to be familiar with before we begin working together."

"Sounds terrific!" Dick replied, "There's no way Jane or I will fall asleep tonight before we finish reading it!"

SuperRetirementPlanner smiled. "Wonderful. It's been an absolute pleasure meeting both of you, I look forward to seeing you soon, and most importantly, I look forward to helping you *retire with confidence!*

Chapter 10

Save YOUR Retirement!

Finertia: paralysis by analysis brought on by trying to comprehend contradicting and confusing financial information.

– Gregory Salsbury, Ph.D. in his book "Retirementology"

(Below is the report SuperRetirementPlanner gave Dick and Jane to read before their next meeting)

10 Steps to Helping You Save *YOUR* Retirement:

Step 1: Don't Go It Alone!

The rules of the game are ever changing. You need trusted guides who focus on solving these special types of financial problems. These trusted guides won't be found in the form of your favorite bank teller, nor at the local coffee shop or beauty shop. The greatest protection available will be with specialized teams of professionals who have both a qualified elder law attorney and a financial planner who specializes in the areas we've covered in this book.

Step 2: If It Sounds Too Good To Be True, It Probably Is!

It's a common and scary trend today to hear retirees who have made poor decisions based on "buying: into "great opportunities". For instance, if a financial salesperson tells you about a 9% CD (when you know darn well the bank down the road is paying 1.25% on CDs) guess what? That's a red flag – a giant waving red flag! When you hear something that sounds that good and you want to believe its true, ask this simple question: So, what strings are attached? If they say there are NO strings attached, then you need to turn and run.

There are many great financial products out there with attractive features, but even the best opportunities come with rules. And these rules are the strings attached. You need to know what they are and decide if they are acceptable to you and are in line with your planning goals. Always use and trust your own good judgment and common sense.

Step 3: Beware of a "planner" that will help you implement investments if no plan is prepared.

Buying financial products without a plan is like having surgery without an exam. Call me crazy, but I sure wouldn't want a doctor to operate on me until he knew what was wrong with me. A doctor who performs surgery without an exam would be an idiot!

The same holds true for a financial advisor who sells a product without an analysis. If you take away the planning process, you are left with nothing more than a product sales person. Do not let yourself be deceived!

Now, a plan may be many things. It can be a short one pager, all the way up to a thick set of charts and graphs. It just depends on how detailed your needs are. Even if the written plan is short, the interview process must not be.

Garbage In: Garbage Out!

The best planning I have seen is not due to the thickness of the plan, but because of the depth of the interview. The planner must ask about all your issues. Not just the ones he can make money on. For example, they should ask about your taxes, education funding, home financing, company benefits, insurance, estate planning, retirement goals, investments, etc.

A good advisor knows how to get to know you, your goals, and your fears. If you feel he or she truly understands your emotions, as well as your finances, then you may be with the right advisor!

I personally would NEVER work with anyone who would make financial recommendations without asking me all the questions about how I feel about my money, and reviewing everything I already have…such as tax returns, investment statements, IRA's, 401(k)'s, insurance policies, wills, company benefits and statements, savings accounts, mortgages, loans, etc., and then preparing recommendations based on all my information and personal goals.

If the people you're talking to or working with don't do this, you should really begin looking elsewhere!

Step 4: If the planner you're talking to charges a planning fee, ask how it is calculated, and how much of the fee must be paid in advance. Ask if the fees are flat fees covering a whole 12 months, for example, or if they are calculated on an hourly basis.

In my opinion, you are usually better off working with an advisor who charges their planning fees on a flat basis, no matter how many hours they spend with you or on your planning. Hourly charges can work, but I have seen many instances where disputes have arisen because of the number of hours being billed. I have also seen many cases where people felt there are too many hours being charged, and then stop the planning process because they feel it's running too much money…thus prohibiting them from getting their planning finished.

Step 5: Ask the planner you're talking to if they charge fees for managing some or all of your money, instead of, or in addition to planning fees and product sales commissions.

Some financial advisors charge for money management (sometimes called "asset management") services in various ways, almost always based on a percentage of the money they are managing for you. These fees can range from 1-3% per year in most cases, and are normally charged quarterly. So, the more money they are managing, the more the fees you'll pay.

This method of charging money management fees is not necessarily bad, but you should know how much the fees are, how they are billed, and what kind of discounts are available for larger accounts; and while this is a structure that can work, I typically find that it is far more advantageous for the planner than the client! Imagine paying 1 to 3% of your savings and investments – every year!

Be sure to get a clarification as to whether or not these money management fees are separate from financial planning fees! Some advisors will charge financial planning fees, and then charge additional money management fees on top of the planning fees. With this type of advisor, make sure to ask them if you pay them for planning fees, if you will be required to use their money management services, or if you're free to invest your money based on their advice with any money manager you choose.

They should tell you that the planning fees do not create any obligation to use them as the money managers, but if you do use them to manage your money, they should immediately disclose how much they charge for the money management services.

Some advisors will not charge you a planning fee, and just charge the money management fees if you let them manage the money. You should ask if they do any kind of financial planning BEFORE making money management recommendations. If they say they don't or give you some sales pitch instead of a plan, get out of there quickly!

Another method to watch out for is if the advisor charges a money management fee IN ADDITION TO product sales commissions. If you are expected to pay 1 to 3% of your money for management as well as paying fees for such things as mutual funds and variable annuities, your investment fees will almost certainly get very expensive. So make sure you're clear how this works.

Step 6: If the planner charges fees, ask if they provide you with a written, 100% guarantee of unconditional satisfaction.

If they are so sure they can help you, they should back up that promise with an ironclad guarantee. The benefits you receive must exceed the cost of the planning/advice. You are the only person that can determine the amount of help you have received...and, the benefit received cannot be determined until the plan has been completed and presented to you. There should be no question in your mind that you have received more benefit than cost. If not, then the fee should be adjusted or returned.

If the advisor thinks he/she can provide sufficient benefit to you to justify the cost, let them say so in writing, and back it up with a written, money-back guarantee on the fees they charge you!

(FYI. They CANNOT guarantee anything about any investments you decide to make through them. It is against the law for them to do so, unless the product has written guarantees built into it, which should be disclosed in the prospectus or other documents relating to the investment!)

Step 7: Beware of financial advisor "employees."

If the advisor works *for* a brokerage house (Merrill Lunch, Smith Barney, Morgan Stanley, Wachovia Securities, etc.) or *for* an insurance company (John Hancock, MetLife, Northwestern Mutual, etc.), you want to be careful. They may still be the right person. However, you need to realize that these advisors almost always have limitations on what they can and cannot do. These limitations are dictated by their home office. And how much does their home office know about you?

As a result, while a particular planning strategy may be particularly valuable for you and your unique circumstances, an advisor with one of these organizations may not be able to help you due to home office driven limitations. And even if they can help you, their home office may not allow them (for various reasons that have nothing to do with you) to use the optimum financial vehicles for a particular strategy. So be careful when dealing with someone who is not independent.

Step 8: Beware of On-Line "Resources."

Information on-line should be viewed with a very skeptical eye. Today it is not uncommon for retirees and their children to get on-line to do "research". The critical questions should be "are you getting information from a credible source?" This can be very difficult to decipher on-line. An additional problem is information overload. If you research the keywords "revocable trust" on Google today, you will find over 3,000,000 articles, websites and "resources" to review.

The problem is, before you finish your "review" of these 3,000,000 "resources" you could be dead and your family would then be burdened by the cost and daytime delay of probate. Obviously, this would defeat your original planning goals. Now, you must do your due diligence and research, but be sure you're researching the right thing – getting the right help. Remember Step 1 (DON'T GO IT ALONE).

Step 9: Demand Proof!

There is nothing worse than getting sold a bad idea. Slick talk can be very persuasive, but in the end it may prove financially disastrous. When seeking professional advice: we recommend that you ask the following questions to ensure that you are being advised by an accomplished and experienced professional. Here's a list of good questions to ask:

a) Are you an author on this subject? Professionals who choose to write typically have a passion for what they do. They've taken time to explain their beliefs and spell out their planning methods. It's safe to say that for most people it's not easy to write a book, so they are most likely very dedicated to their profession and proud of what they do. Plus, you can read their book and then check that the advice that they are giving you is in line with their published message.

b) Do you invest in your professional knowledge? This question is a great way to gauge the prospective advisor's commitment to staying current on new laws, tax code changes and cutting edge ideas to help preserve and grow your wealth.

Ask about their recognized financial designations. Education is an important ingredient in selecting a financial advisor. An educated financial advisor will usually have at least one of the following credentials:

CPA - Certified Public Accountant

CFP - Certified Financial Planner

ChFC - Chartered Financial Consultant

CLU - Chartered Life Underwriter

RFC – Registered Financial Consultant

APFS - Accredited Personal Financial Specialist

The above organizations require that the professional pass an initial exam and obtain continuing professional education. By seeking a planner or advisor with one or more of the above designations, you can be reasonably assured that the planner has made a commitment to obtain sufficient knowledge to excel in financial planning and consulting.

Make sure you ask to see their diploma or certification if they say they have one or more of these credentials. Don't just nod your head in acceptance because the man or woman says they have the designation. There have been numerous incidents where the advisor says they are a CFP or CPA or whatever, and do not have the required licenses, essentially just pretending they did.

If you're embarrassed to ask, you shouldn't be looking for an advisor. This is YOUR money, so if anyone makes you feel uncomfortable for asking to see proof of their certification, then you should get up and walk...fast! A responsible advisor will be glad you asked, and be more than happy to show you their proof of designations!

c) Who refers business to you? It's common to ask for references but we believe that can be a loaded question. It wouldn't be too hard for most advisors to find 3 or 4 people to give them a good reference and say nice things about them. Our question is much different. Where does the planner obtain most of their new clients from? Do they spend boatloads of money on TV ads, radio commercials, and billboards? Or do they grow most commonly from introductions from their happy clients.

Step 10: Be Smart and Trust Your Feelings.

I'd love to tell you that our experience has taught us that as human beings, we will make decisions based entirely on logic. But I can't. People are not wired that way. I recently had a client trying to choose between three local chiropractors. It was easy to dismiss the one who wore really tacky old Hawaiian shirts with mustard stains. The choice between the other two came down to who had more literature available and how nice it looked. In essence, he selected the chiropractor who had written a book, and he was attracted to the book cover.

We've all been taught to never judge a book by its cover – right? But that is exactly what he did. And when he went to the chiropractor's office, his polished image proved to be legit: He had awards and certificates of achievement handing on the walls, the most up-to-date literature and state-of-the-art equipment. He was just perfect for him. He felt better, the service was great and although he was more expensive than the other two, my client finished his treatment convinced that he got great value.

The take away here is: it's okay to be attracted to professionals with well-designed materials. That shows pride. Oftentimes, the ones who appear to be the best really are! Then, when you meet face-to-face, gauge your emotions. If you feel comfort and a sense of greater security, then trust that feeling. Bring all the decision-makers in your family to meet the advisory team. If you all feel that the advice given was in line with their published message, and you all have more peace-of-mind at the conclusion of the meeting, then you've found yourself a good advisory team.

Made in the USA
Columbia, SC
24 March 2022

58122872R00089